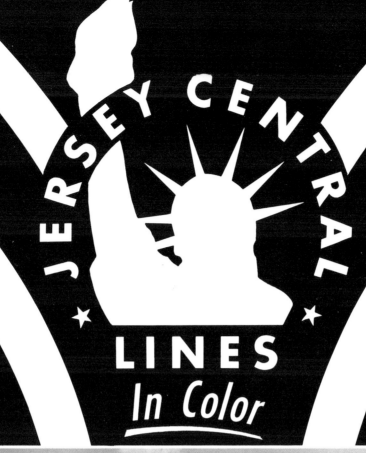

JERSEY CENTRAL LINES
In Color

★ William J. Brennan ★

Copyright © 1991
Morning Sun Books, Inc.

Published by
Morning Sun Books, Inc.
11 Sussex Court
Edison, N.J. 08820
Library of Congress Catalog Card Number: 90-063154
Cover design, layout, typesetting by R.J. Yanosey, Morning Sun Books.

First Printing
ISBN # 1-878887-00-9

Dedicated to Barbara, Bonnie and Billy

Acknowledgements

Assembling this book would not be possible without the contributions of the skilled photographers who shared my interest in the Jersey Central. In this regard, I commend them all for what they added to this endeavor; namely, Robert J. Yanosey, who is also my publisher and John E. Henderson, who accompanied me on most of my pre-Aldene Plan photo jaunts and who shares the photo credits for many of the creative shots we took during thatperiod. I also wish to thank Bob Wilt, who shared his fine western New Jersey and Pennsylvania area material, as well as Allan H. Roberts, Thomas Nemeth of RAILPACE and others who were actively involved in the 1960's and 70's recording the rail scene of the time and in trading slides to enhance the collections of fellow rail historians. Two of my co-workers, Bruce Alch and Fred James provided most valuable assistance in helping me set up a word processing program on my home computer.

JERSEY CENTRAL LINES In Color could not have come into being without the help that all of these people generously offered.

*Most illustrations from CNJ Annual Reports, Employee Magazine-
"Coupler" and Timetables, collection of R.J. Yanosey.
Line drawings of junctions by the author.*

Jersey Central Lines

In Color

The Central Railroad of New Jersey's principal claim to fame in its prime was its role as a "coal conveyor" bringing anthracite coal from mines in the Wilkes-Barre/Scranton region of Pennsylvania and bituminous coal from its western connections to the New York metropolitan area. For a long time, it enjoyed a monopoly on traffic from the Lehigh Canal to New York Harbor and other roads like the Morris & Essex and the Lehigh Valley struggled to construct alternate routes. Until the heating market was pre-empted by gas and oil, the railroad enjoyed solid prosperity much like that of the Pocahontas roads to the south. The volume of traffic that resulted from the CNJ's role as the eastern connection of the Reading and the Baltimore & Ohio as well as its own passenger and freight trains required a four track right of way through its suburban territory. The expectations of continued prosperity in the late 19th and early 20th centuries probably inspired the construction of passenger and freight stations that were much more elaborate and substantial in design than might have been functionally necessary. One can easily understand how the line acquired the nickname *Big Little Railroad.*

****

My first encounters with this *Big Little Railroad* occurred in my childhood during the middle 1940's when camelback steam locomotives abounded. Living in the Greenville section of Jersey City at the time, my family would occasionally go shopping in New York City using the "Direct Line" which ran from Broad Street in Newark, N.J., to the Jersey City Terminal. My mother and I would board the train at the West Side Avenue station for the short trip to the terminal and a connecting ferry to New York. My reaction to the locomotives with the hiss and sputter of emerging steam was a mixture of fright and curiousity, like those of most children.

Many of my relatives lived in Bayonne, N.J., and my family visited them quite frequently. By the 1950's, I would occasionally take leave of a visit while the adults were socializing and walk a few blocks to the Jersey Central mainline. The four track right of way was always busy with the road's own frequent suburban and commuter runs and the long distance trains of the Reading and Baltimore & Ohio as well. The substantial construction of the stations and the elaborate signaling added to the impression of big-time railroading on the level of a Pennsylvania or New York Central and belied the short-haul nature of the Jersey Central.

By the late 1950's I had acquired a 35mm camera of adequate quality and began to record the CNJ on film. A visit to Elizabethport or the Jersey City Terminal would be well rewarded because of the frequent train movements and the variety of equipment. Even though steam had been gone for a few years, the CNJ acquired a fasicinating variety of diesels, some of which were unique to the Central. The sea green color scheme with yellow emblems and striping was attractive and photographed well in color or black & white. In my experience, the railroad was the most hospitable of the New York area railroads. One rarely encountered any objections to photography but, when necessary, release forms were readily available.

The Jersey Central presented the image of a solid, prosperous railroad up to the mid-1960's in the suburban territory. Track, stations and rolling stock were generally well maintained. I spent much time photographing the various passenger operations that were destined to disappear with the introduction of the Aldene Plan in April 1967 when the CNJ's passenger trains would be routed into Newark's Pennsylvania Station. From Brills Junction at the eastern boundary of Newark's Ironbound section, past Newark Airport, to West Carteret on the "Chemical Coast," the CNJ tracks paralleled the New Jersey Turnpike, whose speed limit at the time was 60 MPH. Traveling along that route either aboard a train or driving along the Turnpike verified that the CNJ's trains easily kept pace with the highway traffic. This was even true with the rush hour "back-up" moves with an engine pushing 5 or 6 cars from Elizabethport toward Newark or South Kearny. The brakeman working the back-up hose on the leading coach certainly showed confidence in the skills of his fellow employees in charge of track maintenance.

By the 1970's, the CNJ's corporate poverty was showing through. With the exception of the tracks used by commuter and suburban passenger trains, the rights of way were heavily overgrown with weeds, and freight trains traversing them moved slowly with engines and cars swaying over the low joints. Its original fleet of Baldwin and Fairbanks-Morse diesels gradually expired and substitute power that could be spared by the B&O and the Reading moved in. Ex-Reading RS-3's and AS16's were accompanied by B&O DS-4-4-1000's, H-10-44's, F7's, SW1's and GP9's, adding some interesting varieties of power to be photographed. Two Precision Engineering Alco roadswitchers were leased in 1975 to keep things moving until the advent of Conrail. The railroad itself was gradually truncated, both through trackage abandoned by the Aldene Plan and the withdrawal from Pennsylvania in 1972.

By 1990 as this is written, only a skeleton of the once elaborate *Big Little Railroad* remains. NJ Transit operates a segment of the mainline as its Raritan Valley Line from Aldene, east of Cranford to High Bridge, and only two tracks remain. The elaborate complex at Elizabethport has gone into history along with the adjoining drawbridge. Trackage and bridges from Broad Street Station in Newark to Brills Junction have disappeared. The construction of the "missing link" of Interstate Route 78 around Phillipsburg, N.J., has eliminated a segment of the right of way.

This book affords a look at the fascinating variety of equipment, structures and other aspects of the Jersey Central's physical plant that were quite distinctive. In some ways, however, they shared qualities with those of affiliated companies like the Baltimore & Ohio and Reading railroads whose trains traversed the rails of the *Big Little Railroad*. You are invited, through these pages, to explore the route of the *JERSEY CENTRAL LINES In Color* from the Liberty Street ferry station in Manhattan out to Scranton, Pennsylvania and some of the various branches that enabled the railroad to serve markets that were distant from its mainline.

Liberty Street

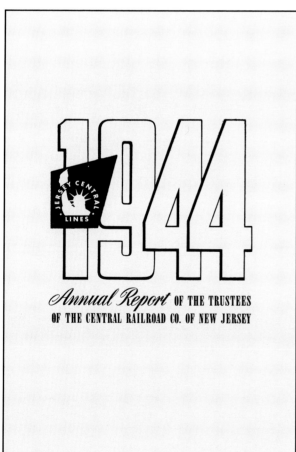

Annual Report OF THE TRUSTEES
OF THE CENTRAL RAILROAD CO. OF NEW JERSEY

The corporate name of the subject of this book has always been the Central Railroad Company of New Jersey. In 1944, a new image was constructed for the company and introduced the Statue of Liberty emblem and the name "Jersey Central Lines." We begin our westbound journey on this fascinating railroad with a look at the Liberty Street ferry station in New York City. Most eastern railroads originally terminated their freight and passenger rail operations on the west bank of the mile-wide Hudson River that separates northern New Jersey from the "Big Apple." The ambitious Hudson River tunnels built by the Pennsylvania Railroad and the New York Central's crossing of that river at Albany enabled passengers on those roads to reach the city directly by rail. Ferries were the other railroads' only options to move their passenger traffic across the waterway.

(Above) As the April 1966 aerial view taken from the railroad's former corporate headquarters at 143 Liberty Street in Manhattan illustrates, the CNJ ferry station's architecture is quite elaborate. This contrasted with the more spartan facilities of the other "orphan roads" such as the Erie, Lackawanna and West Shore (New York Central) which reflected utilitarian 19th century industrial design. The interior scenes *(opposite page)* taken a year later in April 1967, further demonstrate the elegance of this facility with its ornate interior columns, light fixtures and wood paneling.

Crossing the Hudson

Ferries such as the *Wilkes-Barre*, the *Cranford* and the *Somerville* were basic, state of the art creations of the turn of the century with wood superstructures and steel hulls. Propulsion was naturally by coal-fired reciprocating steam engines. Right to the end of operation, the fueling ritual involved short, cab-over-engine dump trucks pouring the black diamonds into a coal bunker below the vehicle gangways. From the gangway, peering through the door, one could observe the massive steam engine at work, turning the propeller shafts vigorously to cross the Hudson and, with equal gusto, reversing to slow the boat's approach to the ferry slip. This is the process as the *Cranford* approaches the Liberty Street slip *(above)* in September 1964. The *Elizabeth* was the most modern of the Jersey Central's ferries; it was rebuilt from the *Lakewood*, which had suffered a disastrous fire. With a modern steel superstructure, it returned to service in April 1951.

(Opposite page, top) The *Elizabeth* prepares to deliver its light contingent of passengers and vehicles to their destination in April 1966.

(Opposite page, bottom) The *Somerville* churns its way across the Hudson on a clear September day in 1964. Despite its ancient appearance, it was equipped with short range radar to assure safe navigation during periods of poor visibility. This innovation was added to the entire CNJ ferry fleet by 1952.

Arrival at Jersey City

The impressive Jersey City Terminal was built in 1889 just three years after the dedication of the Statue of Liberty which was to become the symbol of the *Big Little Railroad*. It replaced an earlier structure built in 1864. The combination of attractive design and durable construction resulted in unexpected longevity and its continued existence as part of Liberty State Park along New York Harbor in the 1990's.

(Above) The relatively neat, well maintained appearance of the main waiting room belied the proximity of the impending Aldene Plan in February 1967. The terminal was equipped with a concrete, brick and steel headhouse in 1914 to receive ferry passengers at two levels to accommodate rush hour volume.

(Opposite page, top) The upper level ferry entrance to the terminal permitted quicker passage to the train gates than the lower level which directed passengers through the more crowded concourse level and waiting room. At the end of ferry operations, only the *Elizabeth* offered access to this level. The railroad anticipated the end of ferry operations for a number of years and arranged for the lease of the small, all steel diesel powered ferries that ran from 69th Street in Brooklyn to the St. George terminal on Staten Island, New York until the Verrazano Narrows Bridge opened in 1964. With the opening of the bridge, these ferries became redundant and available for an economical lease, a better alternative than extensive repairs to the CNJ's own 1900's vintage steam powered boats that were nearing the end of their service lives.

(Opposite page, bottom) Early in the afternoon rush hour in May 1965, the *Tides*, a veteran of Brooklyn - Staten Island service, approached the Jersey City slip.

Jersey City Terminal

TRACK 9

8-12P.M.
RARITAN CLOCKER

WEST 8TH ST. (BAYONNE)
ELIZABETHPORT
ELIZABETH
ROSELLE-ROSELLE Pk.
CRANFORD
WESTFIELD
PLAINFIELD
DUNELLEN
BOUND BROOK
SOMERVILLE
RARITAN

Served Up

Quality foods by Stouffer's. Quality a

Through the decades the Jersey Central continued to make improvements to the terminal like the color coded track numbers introducted in 1954 to indicate the destination of the train on each track. Green and red indicated a main line train to Raritan.

(Left) Like faithful sentries in the night, the track gates and route signs guarded the entry to a late night RARITAN CLOCK-ER in 1963.

(Opposite page, top) The elegant Bush trainsheds, which replaced the original arch style shelter in 1914, frame the soon to depart WALL STREET as its idling FP7s led by 900 await the conductor's signal in January 1966. This consist is one of the very few in the Northeast whose locomotives and cars changed little in appearance from the early 1950's to Conrail's formation in April 1976.

(Opposite page, bottom) Two CNJ commuter trains similarly prepare to carry their hundreds of passengers to suburbia on a route that would not survive the imminent spring timetable change of 1967. The massive Fairbanks Morse Train Masters were the mainstays of the longest trains, easily accelerating twelve steel cars out of a station stop or speed restriction. The use of two separate words appears to have been an effort to avoid a trademark conflict with the Lionel Corporation which offered a line of *Trainmaster* transformers to power their electric trains. The 1954 introduction of Lionel's superb model of the H24-66 Train Master indicates that there was no conflict. Lionel's model is considered by many knowledgeable train collectors to be the most powerful diesel in its line, reflecting the prototype's status as the most powerful roadswitcher of its time.

Tower A

Tower A controlled the final approach to the terminal directing trains from the incoming four track mainline to the assigned terminal tracks. The tower also controlled the moves of empty trains backing into the coach yard. *(Above)* Train Master 2413 awaits its opportunity to leave the consist of the morning CRUSADER to the care of the cleanup crews and the car washer at Tower C, while GP7 1529 waits with a late morning commuter train. The CNJ's Train Masters handled this Philadelphia train as well as the Saturday WALL STREET for several months in the summer of 1964 as part of a locomotive mileage balancing agreement between the Jersey Central and the Reading. *(Below)* On a clear March day in 1966, the WALL STREET concludes its journey of 90.2 miles from Reading Terminal in Philadelphia. The FP7's and the mix of streamlined and semi streamlined coaches, like the CRUSADER, constituted "commuters' streamliners," adding a touch of class to the rush hours.

The CNJ's policy of cooperating with rail photographers made liability releases easy to obtain. Such a release was absolutely necessary to gain access to the vantage point of the adjoining two photos, which show some of the complex trackwork and signaling on the final approach to the terminal. *(Above)* On a hot, hazy July afternoon in 1966, Reading 903 and a fellow FP7 accelerate the CRUSADER on a fast trip across the Garden State to Philadelphia. *(Below)* CNJ RS3 1550 emerges less energetically with a two car mainline local.

Communipaw

The Jersey Central's engine servicing facility was about one mile west of the passenger terminal and acquired its name from Communipaw Avenue, a busy Jersey City thoroughfare that ran from the railroad's tracks to the Hackensack River. The name originated from an Indian tribe that inhabited the area when Dutch settlers arrived. The terminal hosted a wide variety of Jersey Central, Reading and Baltimore & Ohio power for many years and later, diesels from the Norfolk & Western and Chesapeake & Ohio. According to a number of employees of other railroads with whom the author discussed the subject, the CNJ enjoyed an excellent reputation for locomotive maintenance. The skill of the road's mechanical forces was evident from the longevity of the CNJ's Baldwin DR4-4-1500 "babyface" road units. They outlasted all other Baldwin cab units except for the ex New York Central RF16 "sharknoses" that saw service on the Monongahela Railway and the Delaware & Hudson. The author visited Communipaw quite often during the 1960's and it was a rare occurrence when one or more of the "babyfaces" did not occupy a stall in the roundhouse. The talents of the roundhouse forces were equally taxed by the road's own Fairbanks Morse roadswitchers as well as the hand me downs from the B&O, such as H16-44 6701 in October 1967 *(above)*. With the addition of Alco and EMD products, maintaining the parts and supply inventory that must have presented quite a challenge. The variety that must have been the bane of the motive power department, however, created a Mecca for the rail historian. *(Opposite page, top)* In the company of an RS3, F3 56 awaits its next assignment in January 1965. *(Opposite page, bottom)* B&O FA2 4024 idles alongside the roundhouse on an October night in 1964 as a GP30 and a "babyface" share the ready tracks.

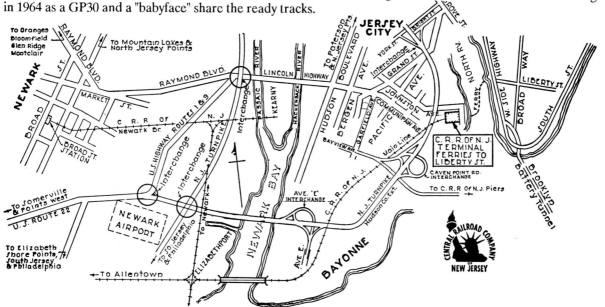

Visiting Power at Communipaw

Power from the CNJ's affiliates and western connections frequently visited the Communipaw engine terminal in the late 1960's. The Baltimore & Ohio was using a number of hand-me down Chesapeake & Ohio diesels to augment its own road fleet.

(Above) C&O 7054 rests in the company of a B&O "torpedo boat" passenger GP9 on a sunny July day in 1968. The progression continued as leased older power from the B&O and other roads supplemented the CNJ's own aging units.

(Opposite page, top) In October 1967 H15-44 1511 shares roundhouse space with a leased N&W F7 (ex Wabash) which probably gave the mechanical forces a sense of *deja vu,* working on EMD F units once again.

*(Opposite page, bottom)*The Jersey Central has "adopted" B&O 6700 as its #19, which is working the Jersey City freight yards with CNJ 1511 in May 1968. The original Jersey Central unit, which represents the earliest production of the handsome FM hood units, has all of the embellishments intended by designer Raymond Loewy. By comparison, the newer ex B&O unit is a bit more spartan, reflecting the effects of production economics. In the author's opinion, these engines had the most "complete" appearance of all of the midsized roadswitchers of their era.

(Above James C. Herold, Robert J.Yanosey collection)

2004

In 1947-48, the Jersey Central bought its first passenger cab units, passing by the EMD E7, Alco PA-1 and other popular models in favor of the Baldwin DRX-6-4-2000. One might wonder if this choice was the result of strict loyalty to Eddystone, the birthplace of the road's later steam power or Baldwin's willingness to adapt its passenger unit to the needs of the *Big Little Railroad*. The resulting "double-enders" were unique to the CNJ and enjoyed a relatively short service life, being retired by April 1958. Reliable sources report that their 8 cylinder De La Vergne engines were removed, creating a supply of engine blocks, crankshafts and other spare parts to add some longevity to their baby-faced relatives in freight service. One of these units, the 2004 escaped dismantling and survived as a rather photogenic steam heater car until the 1960's.

(Above) For a period in July 1964 it provided heat for buildings at the foot of Johnston Avenue, adjoining the Jersey City passenger terminal.

(Opposite page, top) Outside the Communipaw roundhouse, #2004 looks fairly presentable in March 1963.

(Opposite page, bottom) Inside the roundhouse a year and a half later in October 1964, the unit has accumulated considerable grime.

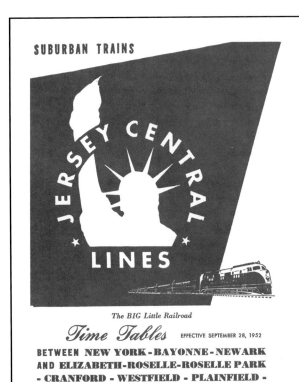

SUBURBAN TRAINS

JERSEY CENTRAL LINES

The BIG Little Railroad

Time Tables EFFECTIVE SEPTEMBER 28, 1952

BETWEEN NEW YORK - BAYONNE - NEWARK AND ELIZABETH - ROSELLE - ROSELLE PARK - CRANFORD - WESTFIELD - PLAINFIELD - BOUND BROOK - SOMERVILLE - RARITAN

AVOID WASTE · KEEP THIS TIME TABLE

Tower C

(Opposite page, top) FP7 901 and the Reading's eastbound WALL STREET near the end of their journey, passing a cut of hopper cars of coal, a vestige of the lucrative coal traffic that made the CNJ so prosperous in past years. Tower C in the background once controlled the Newark and New York Branch, the old "Direct Line" that once extended through South Kearny to Broad Street Station in Newark. This line will be discussed later in the book as part of the story of the CNJ's branchlines.

(Opposite page, bottom) Baldwin RS12 1207 pulls a cut of coaches past the tower and through the car washer a few weeks before the Aldene Plan became effective on April 30, 1967. While these locomotives were purchased for passenger service on the Sound Shore Branch and other local passenger operations, in later years they performed local freight and switching chores such as this.

(Above) The Jersey Central owned the fastest geared Train Masters built (65:18 gearing) and the condition of the road's mainline trackage allowed ample opportunities for these massive, handsome machines to flex their muscles with long passenger trains. While they probably had little opportunity to reach their design maximum speed of 80 MPH, they could effortlessly propel a dozen steel cars at well over 60. After the Aldene Plan, when the CNJ's shore trains used the Pennsylvania's mainline between Newark and Rahway, N. J., the author expected to see these units run at full throttle. The Pennsy's trackage between New York and Washington was being upgraded to form the Northeast Corridor where the high-speed *Metroliners* would operate. Alas, this hope was not to materialize as cab signal limitations restricted the CNJ trains to about 60 MPH and they often ran on the local tracks. About one mile out of the Jersey City Terminal, 2410 leads a consist westbound under the Holland Tunnel Extension of the New Jersey Turnpike and the National Docks Branch of the Lehigh Valley Railroad on a June 1965 morning.

Van Nostrand Place

West of the Van Nostrand Place station in Jersey City, about two miles out of the terminal, the tracks from the huge Jersey City freight yard joined the passenger mainline. Managing to insert some freight traffic through the busy commuter rush hour was no mean task for the CNJ's dispatchers.

(Opposite page, top) The engineer extends a friendly wave from Train Master 2413 speeding a long consist through the Van Nostrand Place station on a hazy summer morning as a freight awaits an opportunity to work its way through the crossovers to the westbound main tracks.

(Opposite page, bottom) The camaraderie continues as RS3 1555 in the spartan solid green scheme rolls its train under the Lehigh Valley main, a short distance east of the station.

(Above) As the commuter parade was beginning to subside, SW1 1010 worked its way westbound with cars for local industries. The engine was a constant reminder of the frequency and call letters of a prominent New York City news radio station, 1010 WINS. All of these photos were taken in July 1966.

DAYLIGHT SAVING TIME WESTBOUND		**Saturdays Only** Except as Noted									
VI STATIONS	633	2785	701	1401 DE	1101 DE	3353 DE	1405 DE	601	1253	1409 DE	325 DE
NEW YORK......Leave Liberty-Cortlandt St....	AM 12.01	AM 12.01	AM 12.15	AM 1.05	AM 3.00	AM 3.00	AM 6.00	AM 6.45	AM 6.50	AM 7.00	AM
Jersey City Terminal....	12.13	12.13	12.28	1.17	3.30	3.32	6.12	6.57	7.03	7.12	7.
Communipaw......									7.07		
Claremont........									7.09		
Van Nostrand Place......					3.39		6.20		7.11		7.
Greenville........									7.13		
East 45th St.					3.42				7.17		
East 33d St. ⎱ Bay-onne					3.44		6.25		7.20		
East 22d St. ⎰			12.38		3.47		6.27		7.23		
West 8th St.			12.25	12.41	1.27	3.54		6.32		7.27	7.25 7.3
Newark (Broad St.)...Lv.								‡6.15	‡6.43		‡7.13
Kearny............Lv.											
Elizabethport......			12.32	12.47	1.33	4.01	3.53	6.40	7.10	7.34	7.32 7.
Spring Street......											
Elizabeth........	12.32	12.38	12.55	1.37	4.13		6.45	7.13		7.39	
Elmora Avenue......			12.58			4.16		6.48			7.42
Lorraine........											
Roselle—Roselle Park...		12.45	1.02	1.41	4.23		6.51		7.46		
Aldene..........								6.53		7.49	
Cranford........		12.51	1.07	1.45	4.30		6.56		7.53		
Garwood........		12.54	1.10	1.48	4.36		6.59		7.57		
Westfield........		12.43	12.58	1.14	1.51	4.44		7.05		8.02	
Fanwood—Scotch Plains..		1.03	1.19	1.56	4.49		7.10		8.07		
Netherwood, Plainfield..		1.06	1.22	1.59	4.52		7.13		8.10		
Plainfield-North Plainfield	12.51	1.14	1.31	2.02	5.04		7.21	7.27		8.14	
Grant Ave., Plainfield....		1.17	1.34	2.05	5.07		7.24		8.17		
Clinton Ave., Plainfield...		1.19	1.36	2.07	5.09		7.27		8.19		
Dunellen........	12.57	1.22	1.40	2.10	5.13		7.31		8.22		
Middlesex........				2.13			7.36		8.26		
Bound Brook..........	1.04			2.17	5.27		7.42	7.37		8.31	
Manville—Finderne......					5.33		7.48		8.36		
Somerville........				2.25	5.49		7.58		8.42		
Raritan..........				2.28	5.53		8.10		8.46		
Arrive	AM	AM	AM	AM	AM	AM	AM	AM	AM	AM	AM

Note, left side of table: "Will not run May 31 or July 5." / "Will run only May 31 and July 5." / "Will not run May 31 or July 5."

‡—Leaving time of connecting train; change at Elizabethport.
DE—Diesel Electric Power regularly assigned to this train.

Greenville

Greenville was the southernmost locality in Jersey City and a diverse ethnic neighborhood where the author resided from 1961 to 1971, an excellent time to observe and photograph the CNJ in the diesel years.

(Above) Exhaust smoke and road grime can make a Budd RDC car more colorful than one might ordinarily expect. Ex New York, Susquehanna & Western RDC1 561 and a companion smoke it up as lustily as any Alco PA as they pass Bay View Cemetery between the Van Nostrand Place and Greenville stations in Jersey City. In 1958, the cash-short Susquehanna sold its RDC1's M1 to M4 to the CNJ and they became 558 to 561 on the roster of their new owner.

(Opposite page, top) GP7 1524 approaches the Greenville station with a RARITAN CLOCKER while a trio of Baldwin DR4-4-1500's lug some "black diamonds" to the Jersey City coal pier.

(Opposite page, bottom) F3 55, a sister F3 and Train Master 2405 lead JA3 down the east side of Jersey City enroute to Allentown. The F3's would disappear from the CNJ roster as trade-ins toward new SD35's soon after June 1965 when these photos were taken. Because of the company's precarious financial position, it chose to take advantage of the more attractive trade-in allowance for older EMD's as compared to other makes. This resulted in the paradox of some of the Baldwin cabs outlasting the road's EMD covered wagons.

The Jersey City - Bayonne Line

(Opposite page, top) GP7 1528 passes through the Greenville station in Jersey City in February 1963 with an RPO-baggage combine and three coaches. Like B&M and C&NW, the Jersey Central selected the train lighting option on its GP7's as the squared portion of the long hood indicates. In steam days the railroad equipped some of its camelback 4-6-0's with turbogenerators on their tender decks to eliminate the occasional dimming of lights and extra maintenance of the traditional system of batteries and belt driven generator on each car.

(Opposite page, bottom) Train Master 2410 pours it on as its train rounds a gentle curve at the boundary between Jersey City and Bayonne in August 1963, crossing under the Pennsylvania and Lehigh Valley railroads and the New Jersey Turnpike's Holland Tunnel Extension.

(Above) GP7 1530 stops for some late rush hour passengers for New York at East 33d Street in Bayonne in April 1967, shortly before the end of service on this route. Its consist is graced by a commuter club car that once rolled through New Jersey's "pine barrens" in BLUE COMET service to Atlantic City.

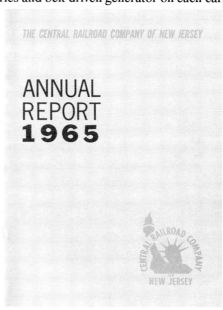

THE CENTRAL RAILROAD COMPANY OF NEW JERSEY

ANNUAL
REPORT
1965

CENTRAL RAILROAD COMPANY

NEW JERSEY

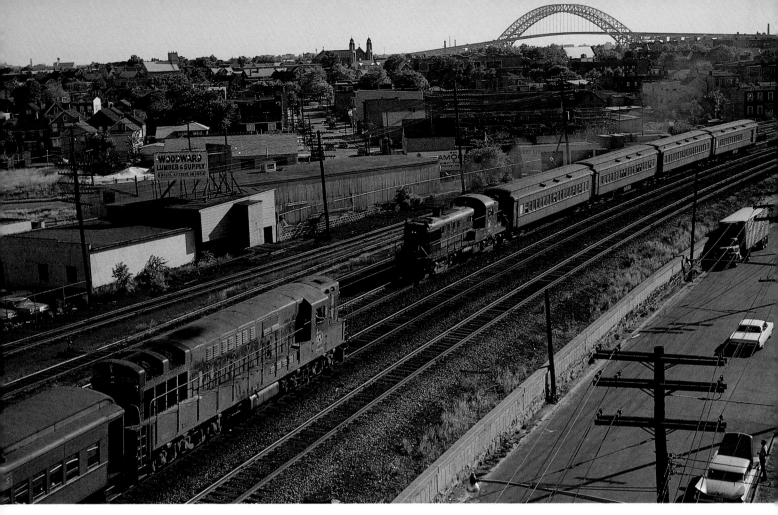

Bayonne, East Side

Named for its sister city in France, Bayonne, New Jersey has long enjoyed the distinction of being one of the safest cities in the country. Exchange visits of student delegations between the cities are still arranged periodically. It was also the community where many of the author's relatives on his mother's side (the McNally family) resided. In addition to visiting these wonderful, congenial people during the 1950's and 60's, the acquaintance with the Jersey Central was nurtured.

(Opposite page, top) GP7 1526 rolls eastbound through the East 22nd Street station in Bayonne late on an April 1967 morning. This is the second Geep on the CNJ to carry this number; the first 1526, together with 1532, plunged through the open Newark Bay Drawbridge into the water on September 15, 1958. When the unit was rebuilt by EMD to a modified GP9, it was renumbered to 1531 to join 1532 in a freight-only GP9m class. The original l531 was then renumbered to 1526.

(Opposite page, bottom) From the roof of the apartment house on East 10th Street in Bayonne, where the author's uncle, John McNally resided, Reading 907 is seen rounding the curve toward West 8th Street and the drawbridges with the Philadelphia bound WALL STREET. In the background, there is evidence of a still abundant chemical and petroleum traffic.

(Above) Train Master 2404 meets an eastbound local led by an RS3 on the same curve with the Bayonne Bridge to Staten Island, New York looming in the background. The overhead scenes were photographed on a clear July afternoon in 1966.

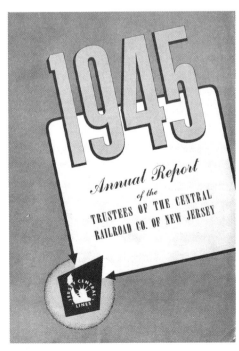

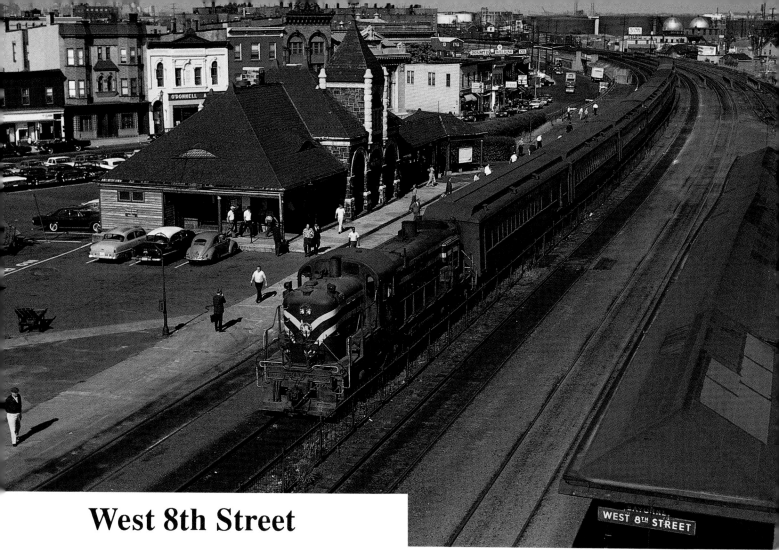

WEST 8TH STREET

West 8th Street

West 8th Street was the busiest station in Bayonne and handled sufficient passenger traffic to convince the Jersey Central's management to consruct this substantial, attractive brick and stone station early in the 1890's. Its interior was completely modernized in 1948. It also served as the destination of most Cranford-Bayonne shuttle passenger trains after the Aldene Plan went into effect on April 30, 1967.

(Above) RS3 1550 rolls to a halt to gather a few westbound commuters at the sturdy stone station at West 8th Street on a July afternoon in 1966 while an FM works the small yard in the background.

(Opposite page, top) SD35 2502, leading an RSD4, adds a cut of tank cars to its westbound consist. It is April 1967 and soon the freights will find it easier to cross the mainline tracks in the absence of the busy full commuter and suburban passenger schedule.

(Opposite page, bottom) B&O SD40's 7484, 7485 and 7483 leave the station behind and begin the climb up the causeway to the Newark Bay Drawbridges in January 1968. Later that year, when the B&O and C&O began to coordinate their locomotive rosters into the Chessie System, they decided that these units could be spared and leased to the CNJ and become its 3063, 3064 and 3062.

SPECIAL **PARADE** TIMETABLE
IN EFFECT MAY 1, 1954, ONLY

Honoring Old 592, last Atlantic-type Camelback in America, which will henceforth rest in glory at the B&O Transportation Museum, Baltimore.

Built 1901. Retired 1949. Resurrected 1954.

The Causeway

(Opposite page, top) H15-44 1511 coasts to a stop at West 8th Street, Bayonne, with an eastbound local as eager commuters scramble to board while the conductor and an impatient commuter wait to alight. BV tower and the massive drawbridges over Newark Bay are visible in the background on this August morning in 1964.

(Opposite page, bottom) Sometimes an inconvenience can yield an unexpected benefit. The author waited in Staten Island for a Bayonne bound bus that never arrived. While walking over the Bayonne Bridge, he passed directly over Baldwin S12 1058 which was working some industrial tracks that ran under the bridge to serve industries in Bergen Point at the southern extremity of Bayonne. The switcher looks somewhat like a scale model in this overhead view taken in June 1965. The Jersey Central route west involved crossing Newark Bay and the ascent to the impressive drawbridges over that waterway.

(Above) GP7 1521 emits its loud characteristic EMD chant as it accelerates upgrade with eight cars westbound past BV tower on an April afternoon in 1966. The train is crossing over Hudson Boulevard (which influenced the tower's designation) as it climbs the causeway to the drawbridge.

Newark Bay Drawbridge

Newark Bay, formed by the confluence of the Hackensack and Passaic Rivers, is an imposing body of water separating the Bayonne and Elizabeth shores by about one mile. The Jersey Central originally surmounted this barrier by constructing a two track timber trestle and swing bridge that were near water level. With increasing traffic and the use of heavier locomotives and cars, the railroad decided to replace the older span with the massive lift bridge pictured here at a cost of $14 million, the longest four track railroad bridge in the country. It was dedicated by Governor A. Harry Moore and opened for service on Saturday, November 27, 1926. It was designed to allow a minimum clearance of 35 feet above mean high water, accommodating all but the largest ships and minimizing the frequency of openings. The height of the bridge required the construction of long ramps or causeways on both the Bayonne and Elizabeth sides to accomplish the climb with reasonable gradients of about 1%. The twin sets of lift bridges provided channels of 200 and 300 feet, respectively. When lifted, the spans provided a clearance of 135 feet above the water. The total length of the main span and the connecting causeways is nearly three miles. Unfortunately, this imposing bridge, like so much of the *Big Little Railroad* is history. The desire of the Port Authority of New York and New Jersey and other government agencies for a wider Newark Bay channel to accommodate the entry of larger ships into Port Newark and Port Elizabeth and the existence of alternate Conrail routes across the bay sealed its doom.

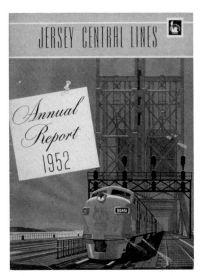

(Above) GP7 1520 coasted eastbound down the causeway from the Newark Bay Drawbridge with a six car late morning train in June 1964.

(Opposite page) H15-44 1513 and its cars rumble through the eastern span of the drawbridge on a hazy October morning in 1963. In the background, another eastbound train is working its way upgrade toward the bridge from Elizabethport.

Elizabethport and the Singer Plant

On the west shore of Newark Bay lies the expansive manufacturing facilities of the Singer Manufacturing Company. The plant's best known products were the popular Singer sewing machines that appeared in millions of homes across the country. The company's founder, Isaac Merritt Singer invented the continuous stitch sewing machine in 1851 and his machines soon dominated the market.

CNJ

(Opposite page) Eastbound Train Masters 2408 and 2409 lead shore and mainline commuter trains past the Singer plant as they work their way toward FH tower and the Newark Bay Drawbridges. The trains were slowing for signals and their brakemen took to the steps to check out the situation. In later years, FH Tower would be renamed "Singer" when all towers received short phonetic names in place of the earlier designations. This practice was common on the Pennsylvania Railroad and continued through the Penn Central and Conrail years.

(Above) A brief acceleration by RS3 1551 releases the characteristic cloud of Alco smoke as it prepares to climb the causeway to the drawbridges and points east as it passes the main locomotive repair shop that proudly bears its 1901 construction date. These photos were taken on a bright April morning in 1966.

Elizabethport Station

Elizabethport station was located where the mainline from Jersey City, which ran east-west intersected the trackage running north to Newark and south to Perth Amboy. The mainline route was originally the Elizabethtown and Somerville Railroad, which was acquired by the Somerville and Easton Railroad as part of the formation of the Central Railroad Company of New Jersey. The other routes were originally built by predecessor companies such as the Newark and New York Railroad.

(Above) In the middle of a March 1967 day, with its light two car local, RS3 1550 will have no difficulty overtaking the eastbound coal train ascending the causeway toward the drawbridges whose clearances over Newark Bay easily accommodated World World II battleships delivered for scrapping at South Kearny.

(Opposite page, top) Reading FP7 900 speeds through the high-level platforms at Elizabethport leading the eastbound WALL STREET while a GP7 waits to cross the mainline with a Newark-bound train from the shore and a westbound freight stands in the Elizabethport yards.

(Opposite page, bottom) CNJ 1511 follows on the same April 1966 morning with a mainline express destined for the terminal and ferries at Jersey City. The massive, elaborate Elizabethport station disappeared in the late 1980's despite the longevity implied by the brick and poured concrete construction used when the complex junction was elevated from ground level in the late 1930's.

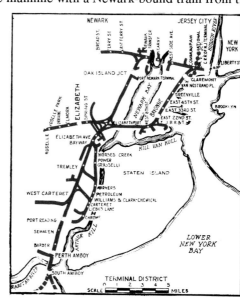

More Activity at Elizabethport

(Opposite page, top) In April 1967, Train Master 2410 backs away from the camera on the eastbound main through Elizabethport with a trial run of a "WABCO" equipped push-pull consist. This type of equipment will prove to be essential to the movements through the Pennsylvania Railroad's Newark station and into and out of the Harrison yards that were nearing completion. Space would be at a premium and the new yard would have no loop or wye to turn trains.

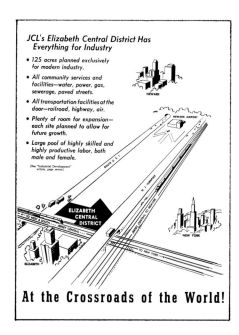

JCL's Elizabeth Central District Has Everything for Industry

• 125 acres planned exclusively for modern industry.

• All community services and facilities—water, power, gas, sewerage, paved streets.

• All transportation facilities at the door—railroad, highway, air.

• Plenty of room for expansion— each site planned to allow for future growth.

• Large pool of highly skilled and highly productive labor, both male and female.

[See "Industrial Development" article, page seven]

ELIZABETH CENTRAL DISTRICT

At the Crossroads of the World!

(Opposite page, bottom) The rush hour has subsided as DS4-4-1000 1073 lugs a cut of cars including some piggybacks westbound across the Newark to Perth Amboy route in April 1967.

(Above) Skirting the high-level platforms at Elizabethport, pioneer unit 70 leads a trio of DR4-4-1500's past RU tower with an eastbound freight; their De La Vergne engines and six pole Westinghouse 370 series traction motors should be up to the task of the climb to the drawbridges that lay ahead on this hazy June day in 1965.

(Above- Matthew Herson, William J.Brennan collection)

The Locomotive Shop

Elizabethport was the principal car and locomotive repair facility on the Jersey Central. The locomotive shop, built in 1901, was extensively reconstructed in 1948 and equipped for diesel locomotive repairs.

(Opposite page, top) Baldwin S12 1055 emits a bit of oil smoke as it idles outside the shop. Its front radiator is partially covered in deference to the weather to be expected in February 1968.

(Opposite page, bottom) A more venerable Baldwin relative, CNJ's last VO660 1043 awaits the attention of the CNJ's skilled shop forces on a September night in 1968.

(Above) The railroad's first RSD4 #1601 rests outside the shop building alongside leased N&W F7 3690. The open hood doors indicate that some more inspection and/or repairs are in order. While these luggers worked primarily in Pennsylvania on the Lehigh & Susquehanna lines and the Allentown hump, they occasionally found their way to the eastern end of the system.

Spring Street, Elizabeth

Spring Street station was located about halfway between the Elizabethport and Broad Street, Elizabeth stations.

(Above) RS3 #1549 rolls its midday Saturday local past GW tower and the blacktop platform at Spring Street, Elizabeth in April 1967. The innocuous street name belies the fact that the thoroughfare that the train is crossing is really combined U.S. Routes 1 & 9, one of the busiest highways in the area.

(Opposite page, top) The 671 series bus engines that power RDC 555 and a companion eastbound are smoking it up as a late Saturday morning local approaches Spring Street from the west in February 1966.

(Opposite page, bottom) Train Master 2405 with a companion that was recently painted in the austerity color scheme roll a freight through the same location in March 1966. The train is using eastbound track 2 that was lowered at the crossing under the Pennsylvania Railroad's mainline at Broad Street station in Elizabeth to accommodate high cars such as piggybacks.

Annual Report 1958

THE CENTRAL RAILROAD COMPANY OF NEW JERSEY

Vintage Cabs at Elizabeth

(Opposite page, top) Five leased F7's from the B&O and the N&W, led by F7 12, back toward their train and prepare to leave Elizabethport yards with the assembled tonnage in April 1970. The lead unit was originally B&O 4577, built in January 1952, by which time the CNJ's purchases were primarily GP7's and RS3's. At the right, an eastbound freight waits, probably setting out cars for the branches to Newark or Perth Amboy and points south.

(Opposite page, bottom) Over two years earlier, a quartet of DR4-4-1500's led by #72 move a mixed consist of empty box cars, cement hoppers and tank cars that typified the non-coal traffic on the CNJ. The CNJ was Baldwin's first customer for these unusual units and, probably because of its skill in maintenance, the last to operate them. While the eight cylinder De La Vergne diesel engine and the six pole Westinghouse traction motors were quite rugged, the "baby faces" had their "Achilles' Heels." For example, the placement of the electrical cabinets under the radiator cores at the rear of the units resulted in some "fireworks" when leaks occurred as they often do in the cooling systems of automobiles and trucks. It is ironic to think that these units were still in service in January 1966 after all of the F3's had disappeared from the system as trade-in material toward the SD35's.

(Above) More leased F7's led by N&W 3697 haul another westbound freight around the curve on high clearance track 2 toward Broad Street, Elizabeth on a September afternoon in 1968.

ENCOMPASSING ALL

ANYTHING   ANYBODY

W   AMERICAN RAILROADS   E

ANY TIME   ANYWHERE

S

for the ASSOCIATION OF AMERICAN RAILROADS

Broad Street, Elizabeth

The Union County seat of Elizabeth is 11.5 miles out of the Jersey City Terminal and five miles south of Newark. The mainlines of the Jersey Central and Pennsylvania Railroads crossed at a site near the center of town known locally as "the Arch." This name originated from the stone arch bridge that carries the Pennsy tracks over Grand Street. Elizabeth provided the Jersey Central with substantial passenger traffic that justified the construction of an elegant brick and stone station in 1891. The station was reported to be inspired by the Canadian Pacific Railroad's Windsor Station in Montreal, another ambitious gesture that typified the *Big Little Railroad.*

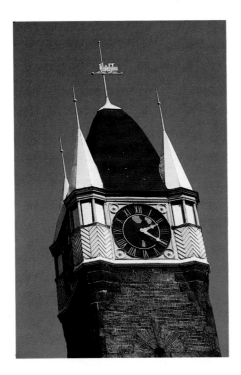

(Inset) The depot was adorned with a clock tower whose style suggested a medieval castle. The eastbound station's interior was modernized in 1953; the westbound side was renovated a year later.

(Above) GP7 1523 accelerates a midday local west out of the station with just a hint of smoke as eastbound and westbound freights pass in the background on the PRR in April 1967.

(Opposite page, top) Train Master 2402 leads an RS3 with mixed eastbound tonnage under the Pennsy mainline with a coating of powdered sand on its trucks and most of the trailing unit on a late February morning in 1966.

(Opposite page, bottom) Reading FP7 903 vents a little steam as it stops for Philadelphia bound passengers on a December evening in 1965. In slightly less than two hours the WALL STREET will roll to a stop under the graceful arch of Reading Terminal.

The Crossing at Broad Street

The heavy volume of traffic on both railroads at this crossing point inspired the author with the possibility of photographing trains of both lines crossing at this point.

(Opposite page, top) In March 1967, the planned photo opportunity finally occurred as Pennsylvania GG1 4916 passed overhead while SD35 2507 and a companion with an eastbound freight awaited an opening to enter Elizabethport yard. Still the ultimate crossing photo remained to be taken, of passenger trains of both lines.

(Opposite page, bottom) Increasingly frequent visits to the site brought the sought after opportunity; in mid-April 1967, RS3 1551 came to a stop as a Pennsy shore train behind GG1 4879 stopped on the bridge above.

(This page) The Reading equipped the FP7's and coaches of the WALL STREET with WABCO push-pull controls in anticipation of using the new coach yard at Harrison, New Jersey, east of Penn Station in Newark. The consist behind FP7 907 sped under the Pennsylvania Railroad's mainline bridge whose narrow walkway provided the author's vantage point for this April 1967 photo.

(Opposite page, bottom Robert J. Yanosey and William J. Brennan)

Elmora Avenue, Elizabeth

(Opposite page, top) H15-44 1511 coasts to a stop with a local train at Elmora Avenue, a mile west of the Broad Street station on a March afternoon in 1967. It is somewhat ironic that some of these units, among Fairbanks Morse's earliest roadswitchers would outlast the more modern Train Masters.

(Opposite page, bottom) RS3 1549 and Train Master 2413 lead an unusual mid afternoon local past the former QR Tower about one half mile further west in Lorraine in April 1967. Moves like this were usually made to balance power requirements and shuttle engines to where they are needed without an additional crew. The tower was closed in 1949 but, because of its sturdy construction, remained structurally intact despite years of vandalism.

(Left) A shrinking passenger volume and a desire by the Reading to operate the CRUSADER as economically as possible resulted in this RDC2/RDC1 combination led by 9165 passing Elmora Avenue. This April 1967 shot was taken from the signal in the background of the photo of 1511.

Lorraine, Roselle Park and Aldene

(Opposite page, top) The crossing gates are down and the bells are clanging as SD35 2505 leads eastbound mixed tonnage past the Lorraine station, about 0.2 miles west of the defunct QR Tower.

(Above) The "Odd Couple" appear again as RS3 1554 leads Train Master 2404 westbound as the midday local prepares to make its Roselle-Roselle Park stop. In deference to these communities' large commuting population, this station, 14 miles out of the Jersey City Terminal, was modernized and remodeled in 1950 as part of the postwar upgrading of the CNJ's passenger facilities and rolling stock.

(Opposite page, bottom) H15-44 1511 appears again, this time near the ramp at Aldene with an eastbound local on a clear morning in April 1967, when all three photos were taken. The ornate vintage milepost pronounces that Philadelphia is 75 miles beyond. When the Aldene Plan (named after this location) goes into effect at the end of the month, nearly all of the Jersey Central and Reading passenger trains on the mainline will climb the ramp at the right and proceed over Lehigh Valley and Pennsylvania trackage into Newark and Harrison. A shuttle between Cranford, about one mile to the west, and Bayonne will continue to use the trackage in the foreground.

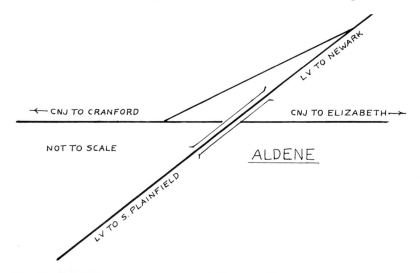

Cranford

Cranford, five miles west of Elizabeth, was an important stop for the CNJ's suburban passenger trains and the location of a freight interchange with the Baltimore & Ohio-owned Staten Island Rapid Transit line.

(Above) As late as September 1967, coal was still a significant part of the CNJ's revenue picture as evidenced by a westbound train of empties led by B&O GP35 3500 and GP30 6916 (still displaying the "sunburst" color scheme that its class introduced) passing the high-level platforms at Cranford. This station was constructed in 1929 with the railroad's first high-level platforms. It presaged the prewar construction program that created the impressive network of interconnecting elevated trackage and high-level platforms at Elizabethport.

(Opposite page, top) Ex Susquehanna RDC1 558 leads a late morning local past XC Tower east of Cranford in April 1967. The tower survived well into the Conrail era, but is expected to close in 1990.

(Opposite page, bottom) A little while later on the same day, a pair of RSD4's led by 1603 pass the substantial brick tower with mixed tonnage. The outside equalized trucks of these units show the residual coating of sand acquired from their more typical helper and hump yard duties.

Annual Report 1959

CENTRAL RAILROAD COMPANY OF NEW JERSEY

Fanwood - Scotch Plains

This station, 20.6 miles out of Jersey City, served the communities of Fanwood and Scotch Plains. The two were a single entity until 1917, when Scotch Plains became an independent township.

(Above) Second generation EMD's of two eastern roads team up on ES99, a joint operation between Elizabethport and Scranton, Pennsylvania over the rails of the Jersey Central and the Erie Lackawanna. Despite the CNJ's April 1972 withdrawal from the Keystone State, the train provided access to Pennsylvania connecting traffic and proved to be worth the effort of running trains up the CNJ's High Bridge Branch to Lake Junction for the EL connection. SD35 2509 and EL SD45 3620 pass the station on an October afternoon in 1972.

(Opposite page, top) WABCO equipped cab car 1321, constructed from a 1300 series arch-roofed coach leads an eastbound local through the station in August 1968.

(Opposite page, bottom) GP7 1527 prepares to load passengers on a February day in 1972. The Geep's color scheme was strongly influenced by that of the B&O during the years after the CNJ acquired the GP40P's and SD40's.

(Above- Robert J. Yanosey, opposite page, top-James C. Herold, William J. Brennan collection, opposite page, bottom- Robert J. Yanosey and William J. Brennan)

Plainfield - Middlesex

The next major community served by the Jersey Central was the suburban industrial center of Plainfield, about 2.5 miles west of Fanwood.

(Opposite page, top) Reading T1 4-8-4 2102, no stranger to Jersey Central rails, picks up passengers on an excursion run to Bethlehem, Pennsylvania at the substantial stone Plainfield station in February 1972 as many photographers and well-wishers observe the departure. This trip shortly preceded the cessation of the CNJ's operations in Pennsylvania.

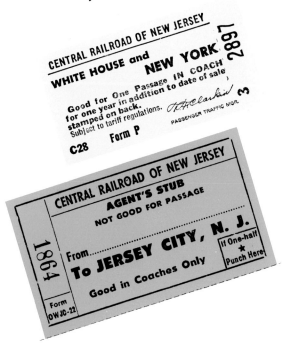

(Opposite page, bottom) GP40P 3677 passes milepost 32 just west of Bound Brook, which we will describe in the following pages, while the author awaited the excursion train. These engines replaced the 13 FM Train Masters in late 1968 through early 1969 and became another CNJ exclusive, among the heaviest four axle diesels in the world. The New Jersey Department of Transportation, which financed the rehabilitation of the old steel coaches, adopted the B&O color scheme in a modified form on the repainted exteriors.

(Above) SD35 2509 leads an RS3 and a leased B&O F7 eastbound through Middlesex, five miles west of Plainfield, in April 1968 with a block of traditional 40-foot box cars that tend to date the photo as much as the motive power. The town and the county in which it is located were named by English settlers after a county in England between the east and west Saxons.

(Opposite page, top and bottom- Robert J. Yanosey and William J. Brennan, above- James C.Herold, William J. Brennan collection)

Bound Brook

The borough of Bound Brook, incorporated in 1891, is a modest sized community about 30 miles southwest of Jersey City. Its chemical processing and manufacturing industries were a substantial and welcome source of traffic for the CNJ. About one and one half miles west of the passenger station was RK Tower and the junction where the Reading mainline swung southward toward Philadelphia.

(Above) Pioneer F3 50 and a mate wait for a signal to retrieve their train at Bound Brood on a clear October day in 1963.

(Opposite page, top) With a dusting of snow on the ground, F3 combination 56-A-57 awaits a signal to proceed in January 1964. On the engineer's side of 56 is a bronze plaque commemorating Raymond Soltycki, a freight checker who was killed in July 1943 while fighting in World War II. These plaques were applied to the engineer's side of each even numbered F3 and to each DRX6-4-2000 double-ended unit to commemorate CNJ employees killed in the war.

(Opposite page, bottom) Low winter sun illuminates DR4-4-1500 #71, the second unit of its kind, as it pauses alongside the Bound Brook station platform in December 1963.

(All- Thomas Nemeth, William J. Brennan collection)

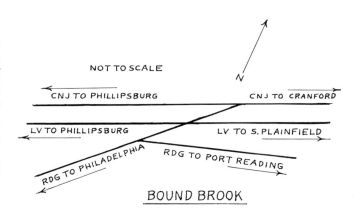

NOT TO SCALE

CNJ TO PHILLIPSBURG   CNJ TO CRANFORD

LV TO PHILLIPSBURG   LV TO S. PLAINFIELD

RDG TO PHILADELPHIA   RDG TO PORT READING

BOUND BROOK

More Action at Bound Brook

(Above) SD35 2507 leads 3063 and two Erie Lackawanna units westbound past the Bound Brook station with jointly operated ES99 in November 1974. The station reflects a Reading design and is similar to the joint Reading-Lehigh Valley structure in Bethlehem, Pa. The hopper cars on the siding to the left are silent reminders of the prominence that coal traffic once had on the CNJ.

(Opposite page, top) The engineer looks back to check out his train as F7 13, once B&O 4581, prepares to pull out of Bound Brook with a short consist that may well be the High Bridge Branch "turn" in February 1968.

(Opposite page, bottom) RS3 1552 idles on a side track as DR4-4-1500 #72 prepares to lead eastbound tonnage out of the yard in August 1963. This babyface was part of the second set of Baldwin freight cab units delivered to the CNJ in July 1948 and reflected some production changes to correct problems that the road encountered with the first trio of units. Among these are the rooftop shrouds at the rear of the unit to keep rain water out of the dynamic brake grids and modified side air intakes to keep moisture from being drawn into the electrical cabinets.

(Above- Bob Wilt, Opposite page, bottom-Thomas Nemeth, William J. Brennan collection)

JERSEY CENTRAL LINES

THE CENTRAL RAILROAD COMPANY OF NEW JERSEY

*Annual Report....*1956

Calco and Manville

Manville, about 33 miles out of Jersey City, is best known for its largest industry, the Johns-Manville Company that manufactured many asbestos products. The durable, heat resistant, non-corrosible material proved indispensable for insulation, brake linings, tiles and other applications. For example, boilers of steam locomotives were and still are insulated or "lagged" with asbestos. Unfortunately, particles of this material in the air in significant concentrations can cause health problems and efforts are under way to phase it out. However, its desirable physical properties are such that it is proving difficult and costly to find substitutes. The town provided the Jersey Central with a fair volume of freight traffic.

(Above) SD40 3063 and F7 17 lead eastbound tonnage out of Manville in September 1968.

(Opposite page, top) B&O F7 4589, which would soon become CNJ 17, passes the somewhat decrepit 1878 vintage Manville - Finderne station in September 1967. The numerous covered hopper cars indicate a prosperous bulk commodity trade that was the major activity at this location. Manville - Finderne would soon become a "blacktop" passenger stop as the depot would disappear.

(Opposite page, bottom) The same four F7's accelerate eastbound past the Calco Chemical Company platform, about a mile west of Bound Brook on the same day. The Jersey Central accommodated certain on line industries whose employees used its trains in sufficient numbers by providing passenger stops directly at their plants.

Raritan

Raritan was the western terminal of most of the mainline commuter and suburban passenger trains. When the Jersey City passenger terminal was closed in 1967, a modest diesel servicing shed was constructed here, about 36 miles out in suburbia, to cover the needs of the commuter fleet.

(Above) GP7 1526 displays an economy version of the red Coast Guard-inspired color scheme as it awaits its next assignment in November 1975 with a "push-pull" consist of rehabilitated steel coaches and another GP7 at the rear in the blue and yellow scheme.

(Opposite page, top) In April 1968, Train Master 2404 idles in the yard with a much shorter train than one would normally expect. In part, because of the desirability of their Fairbanks Morse 12 cylinder opposed piston engines for industrial and marine use, these locomotives were withdrawn from service as a group in the following year.

(Opposite page, bottom) On a Saturday afternoon in June 1965, RS3 1552 leads the westbound QUEEN OF THE VALLEY past RA tower on its way to Harrisburg.

(Above- Robert J. Yanosey, opposite page, top- James C. Herold, William J. Brennan collection)

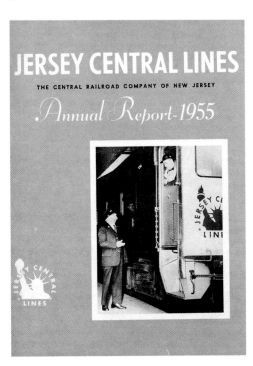

JERSEY CENTRAL LINES

THE CENTRAL RAILROAD COMPANY OF NEW JERSEY

Annual Report-1955

Lebanon to High Bridge

The surroundings of the CNJ become noticeably rural in character beyond the "commuter zone" which ended at Raritan. Only a few "exurban" trains to Hampton, the Allentown and Harrisburg passenger trains and the freights were to be seen in this territory.

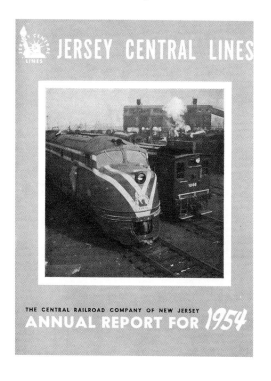

(Opposite page, top) On a clear Saturday morning, RS3 1552 brought train 1104, the eastbound NEW YORK CLOCKER from Allentown under U.S. Route 22 at Lebanon, N.J., in June 1965.

(Opposite page, bottom) This fine telephoto shot captures an unusual combination of the last Jersey Central color scheme and one of the earliest as "Red Baron" SD40 3067 leads rebuilt GP7 1532 with westbound tonnage on BL1 at Annandale, N.J., in May 1974. The 3067 was the only second generation unit on the CNJ to be painted red.

(Above) Freight-only RS3 1704 and SD35 2510 lead an eastbound freight past the High Bridge station on a sunny morning in January 1973 while a track speeder occupies a siding. The CNJ owned ten of these 1700 series RS3's delivered with freight gearing and no steam generators.

(Above and opposite page, bottom- Bob Wilt)

High Bridge To Ludlow-Asbury

(Above) At High Bridge, SD35 2511 and SD40 3065 lead an eastbound merchandise freight past the sturdy 1910 vintage brick station with its fabricated steel trainshed on March 1974. The High Bridge Branch, which led north to interchange with the Erie Lackawanna Railroad at Lake Junction and with the Susquehanna Railroad at Green Pond Junction, left the mainline here. This branch included the 15-mile Wharton and Northern, a Jersey Central subsidiary that ran between Lake Junction and the NYS&W interchange.

(Opposite page, top) The eastbound main track has completely disappeared since being deactivated in 1965 as SD35 2508 rolls eastbound tonnage on the former westbound main near Ludlow-Asbury in August 1972.

(Opposite page, bottom) Train 1199, the Saturday QUEEN OF THE VALLEY passed under Interstate Route 78 near Ludlow-Asbury on its way to Harrisburg, Pa., behind RS3 1552 in July 1965.

(Above and opposite page, top- Bob Wilt)

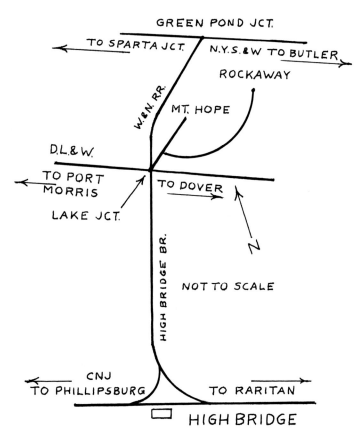

74

Bloomsbury to Phillipsburg

(Opposite page, top) Eastbound train 1104, the NEW YORK CLOCKER coasts to a stop at Bloomsbury in Warren County behind GP7 1522 in June 1965. In about two hours and 65 miles it will arrive in Jersey City after numerous local stops. The eastbound track had recently been deactivated because of declining traffic and will soon be removed.

(Opposite page, bottom) A local freight known as the "Maybe" rolls eastbound through Alpha, a short distance east of Phillipsburg behind leased B&O "torpedo boat" GP9 6605 in October 1969. The air reservoirs were located on the roofs of these units to accommodate larger fuel and train heating water tanks for passenger service.

(Above) SD35 2502 and B&O-style blue RS3 1555 lead a westbound freight into Phillipsburg in January 1970. Phillipsburg is a manufacturing town of about 18,000 people, on the east side of the Delaware River which separates New Jersey from Pennsylvania. It was first settled in 1749 and incorporated in 1861.

(Above and opposite page, bottom- Bob Wilt)

Phillipsburg

Phillipsburg was the western end of the Somerville and Easton Railroad Company, incorporated in 1847, the corporate entity that was to become the Central Railroad Company of New Jersey. The company was authorized to construct a bridge across the Delaware River to connect with the leased lines of the Lehigh Coal and Navigation Company.

(Above) An F unit revival of sorts occurs on the CNJ as ex B&O F7 12 and two N&W relatives bring mixed westbound tonnage through Phillipsburg yard on a January day in 1970.

(Opposite page, top) Freight RS3's 1702 and 1704 lead a modest eastbound local freight past the Phillipsburg passenger station that was designed by the Lackawanna Railroad, built in 1913-14 and once shared by their passenger trains. The Lackawanna reached Phillipsburg by a branch line reaching southwest from Washington, New Jersey off its "Old Main" that predated the famous "Cutoff." A blanket of snow lends a Christmas card touch to this January 1970 photo.

(Opposite page, bottom) SD40 3066 and a fellow acquisition from the B&O, pass PV tower and enter the Phillipsburg yard with substantial eastbound tonnage in February 1970.
(All- Bob Wilt)

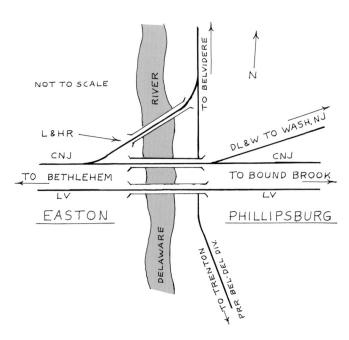

The Delaware River Bridge

The Jersey Central constructed a sturdy steel double track span over the Delaware River in the mid 1920's to accommodate the constantly increasing size of its locomotives and the tonnage they hauled.

(Above and opposite page, top) A Jersey Central tradition lives on as Train Masters 2401 and 2407 lug a solid coal train eastbound across the Delaware. The coal traffic of the railroad's most prosperous days originated from two sources: anthracite, from the Wyoming and upper Lehigh valleys, and bituminous from connections like the Baltimore & Ohio, whose cars constitute most of the train rolling by on this June day in 1965. Finally, the sturdy steel "Northeastern" caboose, reflecting a design originated by the Reading in the mid 1930's, rolled by as an anticlimax to the impressive passage. Similar cabooses were built for the Lehigh Valley, Western Maryland and Lehigh and New England railroads.

(Opposite page, bottom) At about 10:00 on that same morning, GP7 1526 brought train 1104, the NEW YORK CLOCKER across the massive span with a fair complement of headend traffic. Soon after, much of the railroad's mail traffic was contracted out to trucking companies and marginal passenger trains like this one that survived mainly on postal revenues, would disappear.

(All- William J. Brennan and Robert J. Yanosey)

JERSEY CENTRAL LINES
Road of the Friendly Trains

Easton

Easton, Pennsylvania, the seat of Northampton County, is located on the west side of the Delaware River at its junction with the Lehigh River. Manufacturing and cement were the city's principal economic activities, offering substantial traffic to the railroads serving it, including the CNJ. It was the eastern extremity of the Central Railroad of Pennsylvania which took over the operation of the Jersey Central's lines in that state in 1946 to shelter the road's Pennsylvania earnings from New Jersey's taxes. By 1952, the courts ruled that New Jersey could tax those earnings and the arrangement was discontinued.

BETWEEN **NEW YORK** AND
EASTON, BETHLEHEM, ALLENTOWN
PHILADELPHIA

CENTRAL RAILROAD COMPANY
OF
NEW JERSEY

EFFECTIVE OCTOBER 30, 1966

EASTERN STANDARD TIME

(Opposite page, top) DR4-4-1500 #76 and a mate lead JA3 past the distinctive passenger station just west of the bridges over the Delaware River and the Lehigh Canal. The consist includes a fair number of empty hopper cars returning to the mines for more "black diamonds."

(Opposite page, bottom) GP7 1527 emits a bit of smoke as it accelerates train 1107, the RARITAN CLOCKER out of the Easton station stop. Both photos were taken on June 5, 1965.

(Above) SD40 3064 has crossed the Lehigh Canal and is about to cross the Delaware into Phillipsburg, N.J., with an eastbound freight in May 1971. To the left is the interchange track with the Lehigh Valley Railroad and the Lehigh and Hudson River Railroad branches off to the right.
(Opposite page, both- William J. Brennan and Robert J. Yanosey, above- Bob Wilt)

Bethlehem Station

Bethlehem, named for the ancient town in Judea, Palestine, in turn lent its name to the nation's second largest steel manufacturing company. The city is located in both Lehigh and Northampton Counties, 11.5 miles west of Easton.

(Above) The Victorian station is in the process of restoration as train 1107, the RARITAN CLOCKER arrives behind GP7 1527 on a Saturday afternoon in June 1965.

(Opposite page, top) A trio of RS3's led by 1707 hauls an eastbound freight with substantial cement traffic from the Lehigh and New England Railway past the old station in October 1973. While the CNJ ceased its own operations in Pennsylvania, it continued to operate its L&NE cement region trackage. According to authoritative sources, Northampton County produces more Portland cement than any comparable area in the world. The Hill to Hill Bridge that crosses the Lehigh River is in the background; the defunct Fritch Coal Company siding is in the foreground.

(Opposite page, bottom) SD35 2504 and an SD40 roll eastbound mixed tonnage past the site of the defunct JU tower in May 1969. The tower originally controlled the junction with the approach of the Reading's Bethlehem branch into Allentown yard.

(Above- Robert J. Yanosey and William J. Brennan, opposite page, both- Bob Wilt)

Miles from Jersey City	STATIONS
72.12	PHILLIPSBURG
72.49	L. & H. JUNCTION
72.77	EASTON
77.15	E. & W. JUNCTION
81.37	FREEMANSBURG
84.26	BETHLEHEM
84.50	"JU" INTERLOCKING
85.47	"STEEL" INTERLOCKING
87.00	"VN" INTERLOCKING
88.18	"R" INTERLOCKING
88.78	EAST ALLENTOWN
89.33	ALLENTOWN A.T.R.R
90.20	"WK" INTERLOCKING
92.45	CATASAUQUA
94.48	NORTHAMPTON
102.45	LOCKPORT
108.11	PALMERTON
108.42	"HX" INTERLOCKING
110.05	WEST END HAZARD
114.66	LEHIGHTON INT.
116.68	PACKERTON INT.

Bethlehem Engine Terminal

The Bethlehem engine facility was the largest on the Jersey Central west of Elizabethport; here, the more venerable power on the road received the attention necessary for a successful return trip to Jersey City.

(Opposite page, top) On a respite from its duties in the Allentown hump yard, RSD4 1614 awaits the attention of shop mechanics in Bethlehem on an August night in 1967.

(Opposite page, bottom) In October 1966, the Bethlehem turntable carries a rare prize to rail photographers, DR4-4-1500 #71, which appears to be in the process of entering or leaving one of the roundhouse stalls. In 1947, when these engines were built, the insulation on electrical wiring was not nearly as durable as the materials available now and tended to deteriorate in the hot, oily environment of a diesel locomotive carbody, resulting in electrical short circuits and grounds. These contributed to the frequency of shop visits by these units. One can wonder if electrical problems led to this visit.

(Above) In a view that shows most of the roundhouse and diesel facilities at Bethlehem, SD35's 2505, 2504 and 2512 repose between journeys to Jersey City or Scranton in September 1971. When these photos were taken, the Jersey Central was the owner and primary occupant of this facility; that was to change in April 1972.
(Above and opposite page, bottom- Bob Wilt)

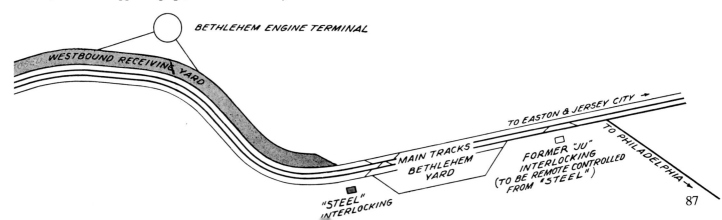

Allentown Yard

The Allentown classification yard was a vital facility where countless cars of coal, cement, chemicals and merchandise were sorted daily for routing to points on the Jersey Central or connecting railroads like the Lehigh Valley, Reading and Lehigh and New England. When the CNJ retreated from Pennsylvania in April 1972, the Lehigh Valley took over operation of this yard, which is still an important component of the present Conrail system.

(Opposite page, top) Near the center of the Allentown yard complex, a quite varied light engine move is led by F7 #14 near VN interlocking along the Lehigh Canal in February 1972. The canal was originally operated by the Lehigh Coal and Navigation Company, which later constructed a railroad along the route, the Lehigh and Susquehanna. This line was leased by the CNJ from 1871 to 1972.

(Opposite page, bottom) SD35's 2511 and 2508 lead Reading GP35 3640 westbound out of Allentown toward Harrisburg with JH1 in January 1973. Pool operations like this continued after the cessation of CNJ operations in the Keystone State.

(Above) F7 #15 leads two N&W F7's and a B&O GP9 with eastbound tonnage past "Steel" tower and the steel welding facilities of Bethlehem Fabricators in April 1970.
(All- Bob Wilt)

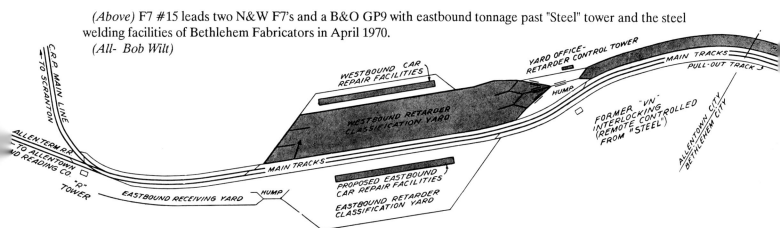

Allentown Terminal

Allentown, 16.5 miles west of the Delaware River crossing at Easton, is the Lehigh County seat and located at the confluence of the Lehigh, Little Lehigh and Jordan Rivers. The city is the major commercial and industrial city in the Lehigh River Valley with cement and truck and bus manufacturing as the principal activities.

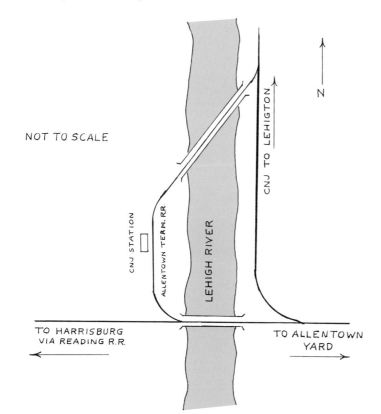

NOT TO SCALE

CNJ STATION

ALLENTOWN TERM. RR

LEHIGH RIVER

CNJ TO LEHIGTON

N

TO HARRISBURG
VIA READING R.R.

TO ALLENTOWN
YARD

(Opposite page, top) On a July day in 1965, GP7 1527 rumbles across the bridge over the Lehigh Valley mainline onto Allentown Terminal rails en route to the venerable station.

(Opposite page, bottom) SW1 1012 switches some coaches in Allentown terminal in July 1964. The 600hp switcher would have no difficulty handling the consists of the Allentown and Harrisburg trains of the time.

(Above) GP7 1522 waits at Allentown to back down to East Penn Junction to resume its trip to Harrisburg with the QUEEN OF THE VALLEY in December 1965.

Westbound from Allentown

(Opposite page) GP7 1520 leads SD35 2505 across the Jordan River and the Lehigh Valley mainline with JH1, a joint CNJ-Reading freight to Harrisburg in April 1973.

(Above) RSD4 1604 and RS3 1555 are lugging hard and emitting a bit of characteristic Alco smoke as they make a pull back from the "field" or eastbound Allentown classification yard on a clear January day in 1972. The westbound yard is nicknamed the "park." In 1951-52, the Jersey Central modernized the yard at a cost of $3.5 million to speed freight movements and reduce operating expenses.
(Both, Bob Wilt)

Lehigh Gap

(Opposite page, top) SD35 2507 leads an interesting combination of power on an eastbound consist of cement, coal and merchandise through Lehigh Gap, Pennsylvania, along the Lehigh River in August 1967. The Lehigh Valley mainline is visible in the background. Both railroads follow the river from Allentown to White Haven.

(Opposite page, bottom) The consist is about to meet a westbound excursion train hauled by restored Canadian Pacific 1286. The bridge that once carried the mainline of the Lehigh and New England over the river is in the process of demolition. That railroad was abandoned in November 1961, except for the cement region and Nesquehoning Valley trackage that was taken over by CNJ.

(Above) By the mid 1960's, the Lehigh Valley and the Jersey Central entered into a trackage sharing agreement because of declining traffic. While the LV mainline remained in service between Allentown and Lehighton, most trains used the CNJ between those points. Consequently, an eastbound LV freight behind Alco Century 628 "Snowbirds" 636 and 634 rolls past the CNJ's Parryville station north of Lehigh Gap in September 1968.

Lehighton - Jim Thorpe

The photos on the opposite page show more operations on the trackage shared by the CNJ and LV.

(Opposite page, top) At Lehighton Junction, about 20 miles north of Allentown, in September 1970, SD40's 3066 and 3068 bring eastbound tonnage onto the ramp leading from the LV trackage to the CNJ's own mainline which will cross to the east side of the Lehigh River. The bridge on the right carried the now-abandoned CNJ mainline that ran north toward Jim Thorpe parallel to the LV.

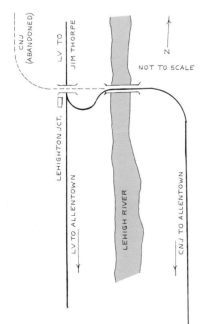

(Opposite page, bottom) SD40 3069 leads Scranton-bound tonnage through the LV's Packerton Yard in Lehighton in February 1968. The train will use LV tracks out of Lehighton until it reaches Packerton Junction, about a mile and one half ahead, and enter Jim Thorpe on its own rails. This name was adopted by the community of Mauch Chunk on June 16, 1954. After service was cut back from Scranton, until September 1952 this was the western extremity of CNJ passenger service. After that, the distinction shifted to Allentown. Jim Thorpe was also the junction with the Nesquehoning Valley Branch to Hauto, which once served anthracite coal mines and brought abundant traffic out to the mainline. The branch also connected with the Lehigh and New England at Hauto.

(Above) RSD4 1606 waits in front of the old passenger depot in Jim Thorpe in June 1969 with a plywood-sheathed wooden caboose for its next assignment to work the branch or the adjoining yard trackage.

(Opposite page, both- Bob Wilt, above- Allan H. Roberts, William J. Brennan collection)

Jim Thorpe to the Mountains

After leaving Jim Thorpe, the CNJ followed the Lehigh River through a scenic gorge to White Haven, then worked its way upgrade to surmount the Penobscot and Wilkes-Barre Mountains in order to reach the Wyoming Valley and the abundant anthracite deposits that once guaranteed the road's prosperity. The 1965 trackage sharing agreement allowed both the CNJ and LV to use the somewhat easier CNJ (Lehigh & Susquehanna) gradients over the mountains.

(Opposite page, top) SD35 2512 leads two siblings past the Jim Thorpe yard on a hazy August day in 1970. The freight operations here were not normally this popular with rail photographers. An excursion pulled by restored Nickel Plate Road "Berkshire" 759 arrived sometime earlier and, while the engine is being turned and serviced, the fans turn their cameras to other available subjects.

(Above) SD35 2510 and companions GP7 1531 and another SD35 lay down plenty of sand as they bring a westbound freight upgrade at Crestwood toward the summit of Penobscot Mountain at Penobscot in August 1971. In 1953, a boiler manufacturing plant was built by Foster-Wheeler near the CNJ at this location. It has since been acquired by Morrison Knudsen as a facility for locomotive rebuilding .

GM
GENERAL MOTORS

LOCOMOTIVES

(Opposite page, bottom) In March 1972, an unusual combination of motive power brings eastbound freight FA2 through Glen Summit, about 36 miles northwest of Jim Thorpe. GP7 1531, nee 1526, was heavily damaged in the Newark Bay Drawbridge accident of September 15, 1958, and was rebuilt by EMD with GP9 hoods and other components. Its passenger train-lighting equipment and steam generator were also removed and it was renumbered to accompany the other accident victim, GP7 1532 as freight only Geeps.

(Opposite page, bottom and this page, above- Bob Wilt)

Laurel Run to Ashley

At Penobscot, the CNJ crested the mountains and began the decline to Ashley via the "back track." Before the four unit road diesel sets arrived from Baldwin and EMD in 1947, only passenger trains, local freights, downhill empties and light engine moves used this route. The heavy eastbound coal traffic was moved from Ashley to the east end of Penobscot yard near the top of the mountain at Solomon's Gap by the Ashley Planes. This system pulled strings of loaded hoppers and other tonnage by "barney cars" connected to 2 1/2 inch diameter wire rope cables up three successive inclines with a total rise of 1014 feet from Ashley to the summit at the Gap. At each incline, a 1200hp steam-powered winch turned a large cable drum (22 ft. in diameter) to pull the loaded cars up the Plane. This colorful, but cumbersone and costly operation was discontinued in July 1948 after 105 years.

(Opposite page, top) SD35 2510 and companions, which we saw working upgrade at Crestwood, are now entering the "back track" at Laurel Run and the 2500's will probably be using their dynamic brakes continuously for the descent to Ashley. The tracks diverging to the left will join the LV's Mountain Cutoff to its yard at Coxton.

(Above) SD35 2509 and SD40 3063 move westbound past the modern consolidated yard and office building at Ashley, part of the 1956-57 improvements that permitted abandonment of the Penobscot yard near the top of the mountain.

(Opposite page, bottom) The crew in the sturdy steel caboose awaits the compression of drawbars as 1611 and a fellow RSD4 prepare to assist an eastbound freight out of Ashley and up the mountain to Penobscot and Solomon's Gap.

(Above and opposite page, top- Bob Wilt, opposite page, bottom- James C. Herold, William J.Brennan collection)

117.79	JIM THORPE
119.18	NESQUEHONING JCT.
121.02	HETCHEL
126.15	M. & H. JCT.
131.19	DRAKES CREEK
132.85	ROCKPORT
137.05	HICKORY RUN
140.89	TANNERY
142.28	WHITE HAVEN
143.81	FRASER E.E.S.T.
147.56	TUNNEL
152.18	CRESTWOOD W.E.S.T.
155.31	PENOBSCOT
156.49	SOLOMONS GAP E.E.S.T.
161.21	LAUREL RUN
166.90	GEORGETOWN W.E.S.T.
169.17	ASHLEY
170.51	FRANKLIN
172.51	WILKES-BARRE E.E.S.T.
174.98	GARDNER'S SW. W.E.S.T.
175.50	MINER'S MILLS
176.08	HUDSON
180.94	PITTSTON
187.17	MINOOKA JCT.
187.56	TAYLOR
190.98	SCRANTON

The L.V.R.R. bracket spans rows 126.15–142.28. The D.&H.R.R. bracket spans rows 176.08–187.17.

Scranton

Scranton, the seat of Lackawanna County, Pennsylvania and the western extremity of the Jersey Central, is 191.8 miles from the Jersey City terminal. It was once the *Anthracite Capital of the World* and the region's abundant coal traffic enriched the Lackawanna, Erie, Delaware & Hudson, Ontario & Western and, of course, the Jersey Central. The city was named after the Scranton brothers, George W. and Selden T. who developed a local iron manufacturing enterprise into a major industry that later became the Scranton Steel Company.

(Opposite page, top) DR4-4-1500's #79, #M and an unidentified cab unit await the next freight assignment east from Scranton on a chilly February morning in 1962 with a dusting of snow on the ground. The combine and baggage car in the background were part of the operation of the INTERSTATE EXPRESS, a Philadelphia to Syracuse, New York train that used the rails of the Reading, Jersey Central and Lackawanna railroads. By this time, the train was exclusively mail and express and not advertised in public timetables or the *Official Guide*.

(Opposite page, bottom) A closer view of No. 79 shows the roof details such as the turbocharger stack and dynamic brake grid shrouds as well as the crew member checking out the running gear.

(Above) The Baldwins have passed into history by the time SD35's 2501 and 2508 pose in front of the former passenger station in October 1969. The CNJ seemed to be an enduring, if secondary attraction in Scranton, as compared with the more imposing presence of the Lackawanna. It was hard to believe that, in about two and one half years, the CNJ would retreat from nearly all of its activities in the Keystone State.

ANNUAL REPORT
YEAR ENDING
DECEMBER 31, 1950

JERSEY CENTRAL LINES

Branchlines - Newark and Elizabeth Branch

The preceding pages have covered the mainline of the Jersey Central from Jersey City, N.J., to Scranton, Pa. The following section of this book will show some of the numerous branchlines operated by the railroad to reach important sources of passenger and freight traffic not served by the mainline.

Newark

As the Essex County seat and New Jersey's largest city, Newark was too important a source of traffic for the Jersey Central to ignore. While its mainline ran south along the east side of Jersey City and Bayonne and then headed west over Newark Bay into Elizabethport, the CNJ acquired a direct route between Jersey City and Newark that was opened for service in 1869. This "Direct Line" served local stations in Jersey City, South Kearny and Newark before terminating at Broad Street station. It left the mainline at Tower C in Jersey City *(see page 19)*. Another line extended southward from Newark to connect with the mainline at Elizabethport. This Newark & Elizabeth Branch permitted through train service from Newark and Kearny to points on the mainline or the Jersey Shore. Service between Kearny and Jersey City ended on February 3, 1946, when a steamship knocked two spans of the Hackensack River Bridge into the water. Service continued between Kearny, Broad Street, Newark and Elizabethport until the Aldene Plan took effect on April 30, 1967.

(Above) The front of the 1917-vintage Newark station blended unobstrusively with the adjoining buildings, giving no hint of its four tracks and the width of its platforms. This photo was taken in February 1967.

(Opposite page, top) Baldwin RS12 1206 waits to depart Broad Street with a morning train to Elizabethport in March 1954. The unit is slightly over one year old and road grime has not yet reached the brake cylinders. The builder tried to bring the yellow stripes across the radiator screening to match the pattern used on the CNJ's other roadswitchers.

(Opposite page, bottom) The Central Graphic Arts Building, just east of the Broad Street station received a steady supply of box cars full of paper from our northern neighbor Canada, providing welcome traffic for the CNJ. Elizabethport-bound 558 passes the plant and is about to cross over Newark's Pennsylvania Station in April 1967. *(Opposite page, top- Richard Pedersen photo, William J.Brennan collection)*

Ferry Street and East Ferry Street

Ferry Street and East Ferry Street, two sturdy brick and steel stations east of Broad Street, serve the "Ironbound" section of Newark, bounded on the west by the Pennsylvania Railroad mainline, the PRR's P&H Branch to the east, the LV to the south and this, the CNJ's Newark & Elizabeth Branch on the north. The partial boundaries created by rail lines gave this neighborhood its name.

(Opposite page, top) RDC1 558 (ex NYS&W) and another Budd car roll away from the camera and over the bridges that span Ferry Street in April 1967. After traveling 0.6 miles more, the train will roll up to the bumper at Broad Street.

(Above) Late on an April afternoon in 1967, RDC1 557 leads another RDC west out of East Ferry Street, 1.3 miles away from its destination as a passenger bound for Elizabethport patiently waits for its return trip. Fortunately, the cars are not letting out smoke that could threaten the cleanliness of the wash hanging out of the homes in the background.

(Opposite page, bottom) RDC1 559, another ex Susquehanna car heads west away from the camera to cross East Ferry Street and make its station stop to deposit any passengers from Elizabethport and points beyond, on a clear October day in 1966.

NEWARK & NEW YORK BRANCH
NEWARK & ELIZABETH BRANCH

EASTWARD					WESTWARD	
		Miles from Newark.	STATIONS			
....	....	0.00	NEWARK			
....	....	0.57	FERRY ST.			
....	....	1.30	E FERRY ST.			
....	....	**1.78**	BRILLS JCT.			
....	....	3 14	OAK ISLAND JCT.	Newark & Eliz. Br.		
....	....	3.65	NEW'K AIRPORT			
....	....	7 24	ELIZABETHPORT			
....	....	3.14	OAK ISLAND JCT.			
....	....	2.53	NEWARK TRANSFER			
....	....	3.31	KEARNY			

South Kearny

South Kearny, New Jersey, was on a peninsula bounded on the east by the Hackensack River and on the west by the Passaic River. It was the site of the huge Western Electric Plant that supplied electrical equipment for the Bell Telephone system. Construction of this facility on the salt marshes between the two rivers began in 1923 and it soon occupied 139 acres, one of the world's largest communications and electronics plants. The facility made major contributions to the nation's military production during World War II. Commuter service to the plant from various points on the CNJ system was a necessity for the workforce of an enterprise of this size. By April 1967, when these three photos were taken, the old plant was nowhere as busy as in former years and would ultimately be closed down and the buildings sold. This train service would disappear with the implementation of the Aldene Plan.

(Opposite page, top) At that time, one of the two daily shuttle trains to Broad Street, Newark, led by RDC1 557, rumbles aross the Passaic River.

(Opposite page, bottom) GP7 1521, still bearing its attractive yellow striping leaves the movable span over the river with a through train to Plainfield. The boiler plant and part of the huge illuminated Western Electric sign are visible to the right.

(Above) Passengers approach the Plainfield-bound train as 1521 waits patiently. The concrete overpass in the background once carried the rest of this line toward the Hackensack River to reach Jersey City and the ferries.

Brills Junction and Newark Transfer

These junctions connected the east-west trackage between Broad Street, Newark and South Kearny with the line running south to Elizabethport and Perth Amboy. The routes formed a wye and small freight yards were located within the triangle they formed. Brills Junction was on the west leg of the wye; trains from Broad Street, Newark to Elizabethport passed BT Tower and rounded the curve to proceed south to the mainline and shore routes.

(Opposite page, top) RDC1 557 and a companion RDC left Broad Street a few minutes ago and are heading away from the camera at Brills Junction in April 1967. They will soon pass under the Pennsylvania Railroad's Passaic & Harsimus freight line and U.S. Routes 1 & 9, and then swing around the curve in the background to head south to Elizabethport in April 1967.

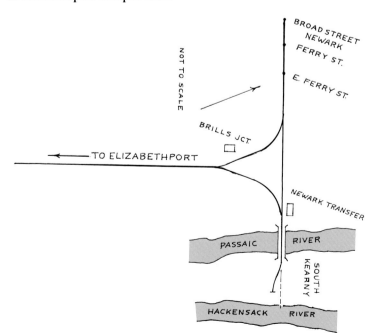

(Above) HH600 #1020 is about to move a cut of cars in Brills Yard, Newark in September 1966. The P. Ballantine & Sons brewery was near Brills Junction and provided considerable traffic for the CNJ. The orange plug-door refrigerator car in the background is one of a small group in dedicated Ballantine service. Newark Transfer and BS Tower are on the east leg of the wye allowing trains from South Kearny to proceed either west to Newark or south to Elizabethport.

(Opposite page, bottom) In April 1967, the evening train to Plainfield behind GP7 1521 passes BS Tower before turning south toward the mainline rails it will use to reach its destination. The Passaic River bridge is in the background.

Oak Island Junction and Port Newark

The Newark and Elizabeth Branch of the Jersey Central ran south from Brills Junction and Newark Transfer through marshland described as "the meadows" which was nicknamed the "mosquito line" for good reason by some employees. Extensive landfill was necessary for any construction, such as Newark Airport, Port Newark or the Oak Island Yard of the Lehigh Valley Railroad.

(Above) In February 1967, RDC1 554 passes CY Tower and is about to cross the Pennsylvania Railroad's Greenville Branch between its Waverly freight yard in Newark and its Greenville freight yard on the Jersey City-Bayonne border. (On page 29, Train Master 2410 is crossing under that yard). The New Jersey Turnpike crosses overhead and, in the background, is the bridge carrying the tracks of the LV's Oak Island Yard over the CNJ.

(Opposite page,top) While it was hardly well known and not advertised, the CNJ provided some rush hour passenger service to Newark Airport. The author once used the mainline and this line to get from Jersey City to the airport to catch an early morning flight and found that the CNJ's trains were cheaper and much faster than any other means of getting there. The only critical point was making the connection at Elizabethport. The southbound train pulled by RS3 1553 is evidently not making the airport stop on this April 1967 afternoon. Despite its modest passenger volume, this trackage was surprisingly well maintained. Trains like this had no difficulty keeping up with or even passing traffic on the parallel Turnpike with its 60 mph speed limit.

(Opposite page,bottom) In a setting that seems to have a rural character, GP7 1525 rolls its southbound train over a sturdy timber trestle past the warehouses, cranes and docks of Port Newark in April 1967.

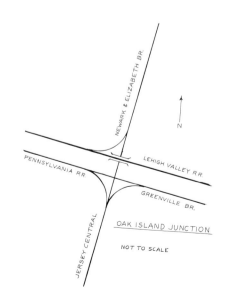

The Crossings at Elizabethport

At Elizabethport, the Newark and Elizabeth Branch and the Perth Amboy Branch passed over a series of crossing diamonds where they intersected the mainline as a continuous north-south route. Four wye tracks allowed moves in all directions between the branches and the main. It was an extremely elaborate junction for a railroad of the Jersey Central's size.

(Above) GP7 1530, having left Kearny a few minutes earlier, takes its train around the wye and onto the westbound mainline to complete its journey to Plainfield in April 1967.

(Opposite page, top) A pair of RDC1's led by 557 clunk softly over the crossing diamonds on the mainline as they approach their destination, platform "N" at Elizabethport on a September afternoon in 1966.

(Opposite page, bottom) A gratifying crowd of passengers eagerly rushes to board the morning through train from Atlantic Highlands at the same platform for a quick trip up the "mosquito line" to Newark's Broad Street station in April 1966. The stop will be brief because GP7 1521 is partially blocking the mainline, a circumstance to be minimized during the rush hour.

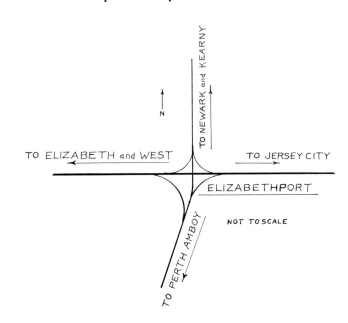

The Perth Amboy Branch

The Perth Amboy Branch extended 11.5 miles south from Elizabethport to its namesake city at the mouth of the Raritan River, on Raritan Bay. The name evolved from its original "Ambo," derived from the Indian word for a large, level piece of land and "New Perth," used by Scottish immigrants who chose that name for the area they inhabited. The city was chartered under its present name in 1718. Until the late 19th century, Perth Amboy was known chiefly as a summer resort, but later developed as a port and industrial center. The branch connected the Jersey Central with the New York and Long Branch Railroad on which the trains reached well known Jersey Shore resorts like Asbury Park and Point Pleasant on their way to Bay Head Junction, 37.5 miles further south.

STATIONS

ELIZABETHPORT........
ELIZABETH RIVER
BAYWAY..................
TREMLEY................
PORT READING......
BARBER..................
WOODBRIDGE JCT

P. A. BR.

(Opposite page, top) Trains from Newark and Jersey City converge at Elizabethport in August 1966. Train Master 2413 will depart first for Bay Head Junction after passengers from Broad Street, Newark make their transfer. A few others leave to board the Atlantic Highlands-bound train pulled by GP7 1529 which will leave about seven minutes later on a hazy August evening in 1966.

(Opposite page, bottom) GP7 1522 passes the boarded up station at Elizabeth Avenue in April 1967.

(Above) Train Master 2409 has no difficulty accelerating its five car consist past the Elizabeth River Drawbridge and WY Tower in January 1967 and keeping up with the traffic on the New Jersey Turnpike on the left.

(Opposite page, top- John E. Henderson, William J. Brennan collection)

Bayway to West Carteret

The Perth Amboy Branch continued south to Bayway, the site of extensive petroleum refineries, the largest of which was owned by the Standard Oil Company, and chemical plants that contributed to the line's nickname of the "chemical coast."

(Opposite page, top) Train Master 2412 crosses the Elizabeth River on the rolling lift bridge on an April afternoon in 1965 with WY Tower and natural gas holders in the background.

(Opposite page, bottom) Another shore train behind Train Master 2413 passes the Reichhold Chemical plant at Bayway in March 1967. The approach to the Goethals Bridge between Elizabeth and Staten Island, New York and the Staten Island Rapid Transit bridge appear in the background. The S.I.R.T. ran from an interchange with the CNJ at Cranford eastward across a waterway known as Arthur Kill to the north shore of Staten Island.

(Above) GP7 1530 has crossed the Rahway River with its train and passes RH Tower in West Carteret on its way to Bay Head Junction in April 1967. The town's name originated with Sir George Carteret, who was granted a portion of the American colony to be known as New Jersey by King Charles II of England in 1649.

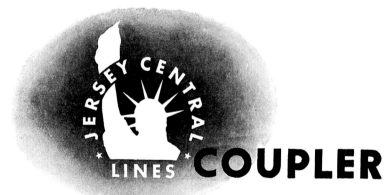

Port Reading to Barber

The Perth Amboy Branch continued south to Port Reading, the location of a Hess Oil Refinery and the eastern terminus of a branch of the Reading Railroad that left its New York Line at Manville.

(Opposite page, top) A shore train pulled by GP7 1527 has crossed the Reading line at "PD" Interlocking in Port Reading, 7.2 miles south of Elizabethport in January 1967.

(Opposite page, bottom) Train Master 2413 is definitely providing heat to its short shore train as it rolls past the small passenger shelter at Sewaren in March 1967. Sewaren is the location of a large electric generating station of the Public Service Electric and Gas Company, the utility serving most of northern New Jersey.

(Above) Barber, the last passenger stop before Perth Amboy, had the most substantial passenger station on the branch, probably because it housed freight offices to deal with the extensive chemical traffic that the area generated. An afternoon shore train passes the 1894-vintage station behind Train Master 2409 in January 1967. At the extreme right, the nose of the author's gold 1960 Pontiac is visible. It was his principal source of transportation to most of the photographic locations in this book.

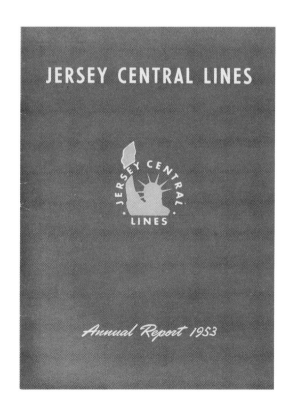

JERSEY CENTRAL LINES

JERSEY CENTRAL LINES

Annual Report 1953

Perth Amboy - The New York & Long Branch

(Opposite page, top) At Perth Amboy, the Perth Amboy Branch connected with the Perth Amboy & Woodbridge line of the PRR. The CNJ was the "first" railroad as the track pattern shows, thus connecting tracks and a "fly-under" were needed to bring the Pennsy into the CNJ station at Perth Amboy. From a window of WC Tower in Perth Amboy we see Train Master 2413 bring its consist into town, passing under the approach to Outerbridge Crossing, a vehicular bridge between Perth Amboy and Tottenville, Staten Island in April 1967. The weather is cooler than normal and the remains of a dusting of snow is still on the ground.

(Above) Perth Amboy boasted of an impressive brick and steel station. It is November 1968 and Train Master 2413 in its new austerity color scheme is an endangered species. The fleet of these FM's will soon be replaced by EMD GP40P's some of which could be considered to be "third generation" diesels. The last six FM's were delivered in 1956; they were ordered to replace the cantankerous double ended DRX 6-4-2000's, making them, in turn, "second generation" diesels.

(Opposite page, bottom) Now on the joint CNJ-PRR New York & Long Branch, RS3 1542 smokes it up as it accelerates past the end of catenary south of the South Amboy passenger station with an unusually light consist. The nine foot width of the CNJ's wooden cabooses is quite evident in this photo, taken in November 1965.

The Atlantic Highlands Branch

A branch extended 10.9 miles from Matawan on the New York and Long Branch Railroad to Atlantic Highlands. Passenger service was discontinued in October 1966. *(Above)* RDC1 553 slowly approaches the empty Keansburg station platform with no passengers boarding or departing. *(Below)* At the Atlantic Highlands station, built in November 1952, RDC1's 552 and 553 await their next assignments. This line originally extended further east to Highlands, then south through Sea Bright and North Long Branch to rejoin the NY&LB. Steamship service from Manhattan connected with this line at Atlantic Highlands pier before WWII. Repeated winter storm damage made the line south of Highlands too expensive to maintain and it was finally abandoned on December 24, 1945. These photos were taken in April 1966.

The West Side Branch

The West Side Branch used a 1.6 mile segment of the old "Direct Line" to Newark, leaving the mainline at Tower C in Jersey City. It turned south at West Side Avenue and proceeded south for about one mile, serving Ryerson Steel, Mallincrodt Chemicals, Metro Glass and other industries on the west side of Jersey City. *(Above)* RS1 1202 switches out some cars at Metro Glass in June 1962. *(Below)* Four years later in October 1966, the West Side local behind the same 1202 pauses to pick up some cars from the Lafayette Branch, a short spur that extended north for a few blocks to serve a lumber yard and other industries in the Bergen-Lafayette section of Jersey City.

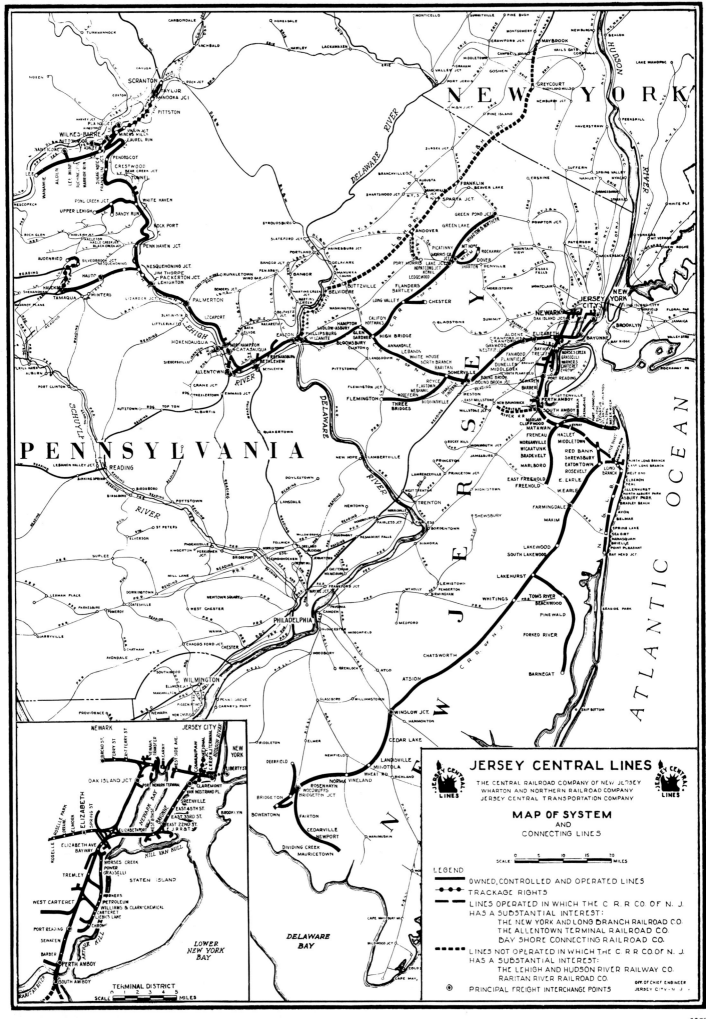

JERSEY CENTRAL LINES

THE CENTRAL RAILROAD COMPANY OF NEW JERSEY
WHARTON AND NORTHERN RAILROAD COMPANY
JERSEY CENTRAL TRANSPORTATION COMPANY

MAP OF SYSTEM
AND
CONNECTING LINES

SCALE 0   5   10   15   20   MILES

LEGEND

— OWNED, CONTROLLED AND OPERATED LINES

••••• TRACKAGE RIGHTS

– – – LINES OPERATED IN WHICH THE C.R.R.CO. OF N.J. HAS A SUBSTANTIAL INTEREST:
THE NEW YORK AND LONG BRANCH RAILROAD CO.
THE ALLENTOWN TERMINAL RAILROAD CO.
BAY SHORE CONNECTING RAILROAD CO.

▪▪▪▪ LINES NOT OPERATED IN WHICH THE C.R.R.CO. OF N.J. HAS A SUBSTANTIAL INTEREST:
THE LEHIGH AND HUDSON RIVER RAILWAY CO.
RARITAN RIVER RAILROAD CO.

◉ PRINCIPAL FREIGHT INTERCHANGE POINTS

OFF. OF CHIEF ENGINEER
JERSEY CITY - N.J.

1958

Jersey Central Lines Diesel Roster

Road Number	Builder	Model	Horsepower	Notes
1A - 5E	EMD	F3B	1500	
11K, 12L, 13M, 14R, 15S	BW	DR-4-4-1500B	1500	
10 - 17	EMD	F7A	1500	1
18 - 19	FM	H-16-44	1600	2
50 - 59	EMD	F3A	1500	
70 - 79	BW	DR-4-4-1500A	1500	
1000	AGE IR	-	300	
1001	DAV	-	275	3
1005-1008	EMC	SW	600	
1009-1012	EMD	SW1	600	
1020-1023	ALCO	HH600	660	
1024-1025	ALCO	S1	660	
1040-1043	BW	VO-660	660	
1053-1059	BLHW	S-12	1200	
1060-1061	EMD	NW2	1000	
1062-1066	BW	VO-1000	1000	
1067-1071	ALCO	S2	1000	
1072-1074	BW	DS-4-4-1000	1000	
1080-1083	EMD	SW7	1200	
1084-1094	EMD	SW9	1200	
1200-1205	ALCO	RS-1	1000	
1206-1209	BLHW	RS-12	1200	
1500-1513	FM	H-15-44	1500	
1514-1517	FM	H-16-44	1600	
1520-1532	EMD	GP 7	1500	4
1533-1535	ALCO	RS-3	1600	5
1540-1555	ALCO	RS-3	1600	
1560	ALCO	RS-3	1600	6
1561	ALCO	RS-2	1500	6
1562-1566	ALCO	RS-3	1500	5
1601-1614	ALCO	RSD-4	1600	
1615	ALCO	RSD-5	1600	
1700-1709	ALCO	RS-3	1600	
2000-2005	BW	DRX-6-4-2000	2000	
2401-2413	FM	H-24-66	2400	
2501-2512	EMD	SD-35	2500	
3061-3069	EMD	SD-40	3000	7
3671-3683	EMD	GP-40P	3000	
3689, 90, 97, 3703, 05, 12, 14, 15, 17, 18	EMD	F7	1500	8
6600-6605	EMD	GP9	1750	9
8400-8405	EMD	SW1	600	9
9225, 29, 32, 34, 38, 41, 44	BW	DS-4-4-1000	1000	9
9700-9704, 06, 08, 09	FM	H-10-44	1000	9

NOTES

1. Leased from B&O, formerly Nos. 4503, 76, 77, 81, 82, 84, 88, 89. Returned to B&O by early 1972.
2. Leased from B&O, formerly Nos. 6700-6701.
3. Formerly U.S. Army, from B.M. Weis Co., Phila., Pa.
4. Nos. 1526 and 1532 were wrecked in 9/58 and rebuilt by EMD as modified GP9s without head end lighting or steam generators. The CNJ exchanged numbers between 1526 and 1531 to form a frieght-only GP9 group.
5. Ex-Reading 460, 461, 472, 486, 475, 489, 490, 522. Engines 1533 to 1535 were lettered for LNE.
6. Nos. 1560-1561 were acquired from Precision Engineering Co., originally Central of Georgia and Spokane, Portland & Seattle.
7. Originally B&O 7482-7490, leased to the CNJ in 11/67 to 3/68.
8. Leased from Norfolk & Western. No. 3715 was repainted and renumbered to CNJ 27, but the N&W insisted that it be returned to its original appearance.
9. These engines were leased from the B&O and were relettered by the CNJ but retained their original numbers.

Farewell

    The *Big Little Railroad*, despite valiant efforts by decades of resourceful managers and dedicated employees, has passed into history. During the years following World War II, the arrival of the tangerine and blue road diesels gave rise to hope that the economic malaise afflicting the Jersey Central and the northeastern railroads could be overcome. Similar optimistic expectations arose with the later introduction of the Budd RDC cars, massive Train Masters and, finally the second generation SD35s. The loss of the once abundant coal traffic, onerous taxation and subsidized highway competition, unfortunately, made the end inevitable. The Jersey Central was absorbed into the huge Conrail system on April 1, 1976 and its passenger operations were taken over by New Jersey Transit. Some equipment has been preserved and many of the suburban passenger stations remain intact, but the most impressive structures like the Newark Bay Drawbridge and the elevated Elizabethport complex have disappeared. The Jersey Central will live on, however, in the form of photos, slides, preserved equipment, models and books such as this. *It is an honor to help preserve the memories of this fascinating railroad.*

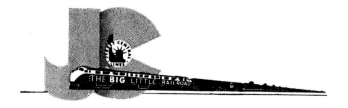